P9-DNP-562

ADVENTURES OF A GHOST HUNTER

Kristin Rice-Nori

About the Author

Adam Nori is the team lead and founder of the Minnesota Paranormal Study Group (MNPSG). The team offers investigation data on their website, MinnesotaGhosts.com.

Aside from his own team, Adam has been involved in projects within the paranormal field, including being a liaison with The Atlantic Paranormal Society Family (TAPS Family) and editor for *ECTO Magazine*.

To Write to the Author

If you wish to contact the author or would like more information about this book, please write to the author in care of Llewellyn Worldwide, and we will forward your request. Both the author and publisher appreciate hearing from you and learning of your enjoyment of this book and how it has helped you. Llewellyn Worldwide cannot guarantee that every letter written to the author can be answered, but all will be forwarded. Please write to:

Adam Nori
⁄ Llewellyn Worldwide
2143 Wooddale Drive
Woodbury, MN 55125-2989

Please enclose a self-addressed stamped envelope for reply, or $1.00 to cover costs. If outside the USA, enclose an international postal reply coupon.

ADVENTURES OF A GHOST HUNTER

MY INVESTIGATIONS INTO THE DARKNESS

ADAM NORI

Llewellyn Publications
Woodbury, Minnesota

FIRST EDITION
First Printing, 2013

Book design by Bob Gaul
Cover art: Girl: iStockphoto.com/M. Eric Honeycutt
          Nighttime mist: iStockphoto.com/Denis Jr. Tangney
Cover design by Kevin R. Brown
Editing by Laura Graves

Llewellyn Publications is a registered trademark of Llewellyn Worldwide Ltd.

Library of Congress Cataloging-in-Publication Data
Nori, Adam, 1985–
  Adventures of a ghost hunter: my investigations into the darkness/Adam Nori.
  —1st ed.
    p. cm.
  ISBN 978-0-7387-3541-2
1. Nori, Adam, 1985– 2. Occultists—Biography. 3. Ghosts—Minnesota. I. Title.
  BF1408.2.N67A3 2013
  133.1092—dc23
  [B]
                              2012035360

Llewellyn Worldwide Ltd. does not participate in, endorse, or have any authority or responsibility concerning private business transactions between our authors and the public.

All mail addressed to the author is forwarded, but the publisher cannot, unless specifically instructed by the author, give out an address or phone number.

Any Internet references contained in this work are current at publication time, but the publisher cannot guarantee that a specific location will continue to be maintained. Please refer to the publisher's website for links to authors' websites and other sources.

Llewellyn Publications   *5042 6971 1/13*
A Division of Llewellyn Worldwide Ltd.
2143 Wooddale Drive
Woodbury, MN 55125-2989
www.llewellyn.com

Printed in the United States of America

Dedicated to Bobby Lusti
and the many people I have met
along my spooky yellow brick road

Contents

Preface

It is 2 a.m., and I am sitting in a dark bus with two other people hoping that a little red light goes off. It is a typical Minnesota spring with temperatures in the twenties and a dusting of stubborn snow on the ground. Most people are asleep at this hour, but here we sit trying to find something to give to the client to assure them that their imagination is not getting the best of them.

We are trying to find the ghostly culprit who opens bus windows and closes the doors on the buses when the museum staff is not around.

"What was that?" Mick exclaims as he points towards the glass windows at my window.

I stare outside into the darkness, afraid of what may peer back at me as visions of previous accounts of darkness scares creep into my mind. Was it a pair of red eyes? A face? What did he see?

"It almost appeared to be like two white lights whizzing by the bus!" he states.

"Make sure it is not your camera, Don. Can we reproduce it?" I ask with a hesitant tone of voice as I am still concerned for my own emotions as well as the validity of the evidence. "Was it the IR light off of our video camera?"

Don moves the Sony Handycam with a special infrared illuminator he has in his left hand up and down followed by right to left.

"No, it was not that. It almost appeared to be like two eyes in the dark," Mick says. "I just saw it for a brief second."

My heart begins to pound. One of my greatest scares is that a set of eyes or a face will jump out at me in the darkness. No one likes to stare outside a glass window and then have a face suddenly appear confirming that you are not alone as you look into the unknown.

Yet that is exactly what we are doing…looking into the unknown.

"Well, if we can't reproduce it ourselves, we might have got it on camera," I calmly say to try to hide my emotional disarray.

All we have to go on is what we might have missed but caught on our electronic devices.

Introduction

It was once written, "Some people tell ghost stories. Adam Nori is living one."

For the better part of my life as a whole, I have spent most of my free time walking around in the shadows of strange places looking for something I have been familiar with for years: lost souls.

Ever since I was a child, I have had signs of placing me on this path to the paranormal. As a youngster in the 1980s, I often played around with a bent coat hanger and pretended to be one of my heroes, the Ghostbusters. I would walk throughout my house with this junk in my hand and pretend it was a meter that could find ghosts. Little did I know how much this would carry into my adult life—and sometimes even with a bent coat hanger!

Looking back on my youth, it still is even odd to me that these signs existed, and I know that anyone my age would point out that many kids were into the Ghostbusters and looked up to them but not many can say that they had ghosts on one of their birthday cakes. As a person who believes that proof is the definitive answer to showcase an experience, I recall a particular photo of my cake from my fourth birthday in 1989. My mother had gone to a store to try to get a cake with the Ghostbusters logo on it. Due to confusion and lack of knowing how to make a logo cake in the late 1980s, it simply featured classic ghosts on it.

Apparently, the universe had stepped in. As it is said, history was made.

While my childhood was one of bent coat hangers and proton pack dreamin', it was in my teen years I learned that people did "hunt" real ghosts, and I read stories of haunted locations I thought were fascinating. I credit my father for helping me find this dream because he always has an open mind about things and we used to watch the television show *Sightings* on a regular basis. The program was an hour-long news broadcast of the weird and unexplained, with features on different stories, many of which showcased these ghost hunters.

I became fascinated with the hope of finding something beyond death due to a personal experience I will discuss in better detail later on in this journey.

During high school, I became entrenched in my desire to read and study all that I could about the world of the paranormal. I could always be found with a book on the matter or some material printed from a website. It became something that made my learning experience in high school relevant and fun because I could always tie the material to whatever class I was in.

If I was in physics class, I could tie the need for that course to my desire to understand thrown objects in a poltergeist case. If it were English class, it was my need to be able to write about my experiences in a document format. Spanish class allowed me to understand other cultures and also talk about *el chupacabra*!

While this all may seem silly to some (including my teachers in those courses), my education enabled me to understand that quite a bit of knowledge was required for approaching the unknown. My passion allowed me to teach many, including my peers and adults within the community, during my high school career. As a sixteen-year-old, I ended up talking to others who were beyond my own level of maturity and understanding of life. I realized I needed a diverse skill set, and it is something I still apply to my career as a ghost hunter.

I led a very bizarre life early on, but I don't regret any of it. I did something different and very meaningful and enjoyed it because I was so passionate about it. Really, that is the key to life: apply your passion and talents to the world in which others find value.

In high school, I founded my own paranormal research team, the Minnesota Paranormal Study Group, or MNPSG for short. I started this organization because I knew I would need people like myself to tackle situations others needed assistance with. While this group started back in the late 1990s at the hands of a teenager, it has become something I take pride in because it has helped others and done some really wonderful things.

The early years of "the group" were uneventful; it was pretty much an informal group of friends and family I would bring out for investigations in public places such as cemeteries. It wasn't until my college years that the group took on a formal approach and introduced people who were dedicated other than me. When we adopted this approach, we began our public website, www.Minnesota Ghosts.com, which gives a raw look into our investigative data from locations we visit.

Our current team has included twenty-nine members over the course of its history and has become a premier source for haunting information in the Midwest. We have documented various urban legends, haunted locations, and more importantly, historical information about the Land of 10,000 Lakes.

The original team consisted of five members who met in Mankato, Minnesota: Monica Zacharias, Nancy Willis,

Garrett Sack, Kelly Garvin, and yours truly. With no direction on how to start a paranormal research group, we dedicated our efforts to finding locations with historical significance that had rumors of being eerie. Even if we did not capture any evidence that would support the claims of it being haunted, we were able to provide a historical backstory on why the location was interesting.

Southern Minnesota has an interesting past of tales about the Civil War, the Sioux Uprising of 1862, the origins of the world-famous Mayo Clinic, and other historical events that shaped Minnesota's history. (Did you know that the small town of St. Peter almost became the state capital?)

Once the ball began rolling, the public took notice of what we were doing, and we started to receive invites into peoples' homes. We were able to help families that believed something unknown was affecting the course of their daily lives.

After my college years in Mankato, I moved back to my hometown of Aurora, located on the Iron Range of northern Minnesota. Many people want to escape their towns to explore the world, and my town was no different. However, I found myself returning to my home area with stories of my adventures. I wanted to dig up the history that shaped the Iron Range.

For anyone who has visited the southern and northern parts of Minnesota, you will notice that they are very much polar opposites in terms of culture, landscape, and history. This difference gave me a new challenge and a chance to accept new excursions into the unknown.

Today, I lead a new team of investigators who explore the haunted history of Minnesota from the city of Hibbing. The team consists of people from various towns in northern Minnesota such as Justin Holley (Bemidji), Kayla Rantala (Aurora), Matt Ashmore (Eveleth), and my wife, Kristin Rice-Nori (Keewatin).

Since our team has grown in the years since its inception, we have received case leads from the public through various means of communication. People can write us an email, call us on the phone, and find us at various community events we are involved with. Some of these events include the Field of Screams attraction in Chisholm and educational seminars we host at various venues such as public libraries. The money we collect from these events is paid out to various charities we believe help others and preserve history. In other words, we do not gain profit for anything that we do.

My original goal with this organization was the ability to hear others' stories of the unknown, and when you have had the ability to have as many great adventures and meet all the great people as I have, as one wise person once told me, that is payment enough.

PART ONE

1

THE COIN PROMISE

"A man's integrity is more important than money," Bobby said.

I listened intently as my uncle told me a story that was made long before my time. I was eight years old, barely tall enough to see over the kitchen table, where he sat holding a silver dollar.

"Your Uncle Milt gave me this in 1974. He was always mad at me because I had no money, so he gave me this and said to me, 'I bet you can't hold onto this for twenty years, let alone twenty minutes.' I wanted to prove him wrong so we made a bet," Bobby explained.

Uncle Bobby was a heavy, stout man with a brown beard and a booming voice. A man without a job other than to take care of his diabetic mother who he lived with, he was the fill-in-father who was there when my dad worked to support our family. In many peoples' eyes, Bobby was a slob who wore a brown jacket, simple colored Hanes t-shirts, and blue jeans. He even wore tennis shoes with Velcro straps as a fashion statement.

In my eyes, Bobby was a hero.

He was the type to take time out for everyone in his life. Born with so much borrowed time, Bobby was the kind of man who understood that life's true value was the people in it, which was apparent as he kept as many around him as possible. One of the people he kept around him was his youngest sister's son; a blond-haired, blue-eyed monster who would one day grow up to tell adventures that were shared between a boy and his mortal hero.

The two of them would exchange life lessons, such as this story about a coin, for the perspective and wonder of youth. Often times, these adventures in life would take place at extraordinary locales such as the grocery store, other relative's homes, and a poor, empty kitchen where government cheese was served with pride.

"We shook on the deal, which means that you are bound to it by honor, and he wanted to etch the year that we made the promise into the coin so I didn't try to trick him. I would never do that to him, as he was my own brother. He carved the year into there. See that?"

The coin had a marking of 1974, obviously carved by a knife. Bobby threw the coin up in the air and caught it with a slight smile on his face. He rubbed the top of my head and walked into the living room.

"A man is only as good as his word. You can say anything you want but if you do not live up to it, what good is it? That's why I don't like politicians, too much talk."

The year was 1993; one more year and Bobby would win the bet.

"What happens when you win?" I asked with childish innocence as I loyally followed Bobby into the other room.

"A case of beer," he replied.

I smiled and cheered him on because I wanted to see my idol claim his trophy. I offered him my candy money so he wouldn't have to spend the coin.

Over the years, this coin became a symbol of my uncle and something he would proudly show everyone he knew as if to say, "See what I have still?" He was very proud of this physical token. In many ways, it was his trophy, a conversation piece that defined his character and let him make new friends. It symbolized the type of person Bobby was.

In 1994, Bobby did win the bet, but more importantly, he kept a promise.

2

THE CEMETERY ADVENTURE

On a day in May, 1993, the birds were singing, the sky was blue, and I was riding shotgun with my best friend. I was eight, he was forty-three. We traveled down a dirt road in rural northeastern Minnesota while I ate a sucker.

I looked around his dashboard. He had such cool things in here. A mini-calendar, which was a month behind, that advertised a local business. A small stick-on digital clock. A dozen air fresheners shaped like trees. Various pens that were all handouts from some businesses. Can coolers that either gave you a piece of his mind or where to go for cheap beer.

He had a style all his own. I envied it.

He put in a new cassette tape into the car stereo.

"I want you to listen to this song because you might like it," he said.

"Okay. Who is it?"

"Travis Tritt."

What's it called?

"'Country Club'."

The serenade of the twangs and honky-tonk came through the speakers. I listened intently because he asked me to.

"He drinks from a Dixie cip, just like you!" I said with a slight laugh.

I thought that was silly at the time and didn't know the real implications of it. Besides, in my eight-year-old mind, he was a member of a country club because he always ordered country tapes through those club catalogs. You know the kind, ten cassettes for a penny.

Even though I had just called him a cheap drunk in an adult sense, Bobby smiled at me as he turned down a small driveway. He always seemed to be on my level.

We were at the Rauhua Cemetery in Palo, where I have relatives buried. Since my dad was always working, Bobby took the time to take me out here to see where my paternal grandfather was buried.

He brushed off the headstone and pushed me ahead.

"Go ahead, it's okay," Bobby said with a calm tone. "If you want to say something, you can say it aloud or in your head. He will get the message either way."

I quietly stood next to the headstone and thought about my grandfather. I had no memory of him; he passed away when I was still a baby. I remember my parents telling me how proud he was to have me as a grandson and always posed with me for photos.

I turned around with a solemn look on my face. Bobby asked me what was wrong.

"I just feel funny talking to no one."

"Your grandpa heard you and is glad that you came."

"How do you know?"

"I know because family is important; living or dead. Knowing who you are and where you came from is a large part of being a good person."

We headed around the cemetery and found more relatives of mine a few generations back. I had never had the chance to meet these people but still stopped to say hello at their markers. I introduced myself in a polite fashion just in case the dead could hear me.

"I don't like walking on the grass and stepping over graves," Bobby proclaimed. "It gives me the heebie-jeebies." He said the thought of walking over someone was disrespectful and just not right in his mind. We almost seemed to play hopscotch in the grass as we tried to avoid invading any resident's space.

As we got to the car, I opened my door. Bobby paused a bit as he looked around one last time. I got back out of the car and looked at him.

"One day, I hope you will come to visit me when I am dead," he said.

"You won't die."

"One day I will, and you will tell your kids about me."

"You can't die."

"It happens to everyone sooner or later. Just promise you will visit and think of me, okay?"

"I promise. Someone has to bring you those Dixie cups!"

We hesitated for a while until Bobby started to laugh.

"You crack me up, Bomber," he said with a smile.

3

DEATH ENDS A LIFE...

"Mom, why are we going to Grandma's today?" I asked, half asleep. It was 1995.

The rain was just starting to turn the sky gray with gloom and foreshadow the day to come. I looked out the window with sleepy eyes to see the green of pine trees blend in with the white of the foggy mist. My mind couldn't process our trip to my grandmother's apartment in Virginia, Minnesota, because it was not our normal schedule. School had just started and it was unlike my parents to pull me out of it for a "fun day" with Bobby.

"Just pack up some of your toys you want to bring along, and hurry up," she said in an emotional state I had never seen her in. "Your uncle Bobby is sick, and we need to go see him."

This confused me, because I had just seen him a few days ago and we had a good time. He seemed to be his normal self and was not sick in the least. I was not one to question my mother, not in this panic mode that she was in anyway. So I packed some toys into a bag and grabbed my mom's hand. She looked like she needed it.

I looked out my window in the back seat of our 1969 Dodge Dart and remember wondering, "I wonder why Bobby is sick? Are we going to help tuck him in and make him soup?" At least, that's what always made me feel better when I was sick…

During the car ride, I did my normal sing-along with the radio quietly in the back seat. I thought about what adventures lay ahead of me and my uncle for today. I liked going to my grandma's apartment, which was on the bottom level of a large white building with black trim. I'd sneak into the living room as not to awake my uncle who slept on the couch with the television turned towards him. My mom would help me pull the television back so I could watch Nickelodeon, which was a big deal since we didn't get this channel in the rural parts. My uncle would wake up and playfully yell at me because I'd turn his re-runs of *Gilligan's Island* or *Bewitched* off and put on something with puppets. (Looking back, I can see his side of the story, but when you only get two channels at home, you will watch anything!)

My dad worked in Virginia, about a forty-minute commute from where we lived. In the summer, my mother and I would tag along so we could spend the day with her family. I really enjoyed those days because it usually meant that I got to watch cartoons all morning, get McDonald's for lunch, and then go with my mom to see what the department stores had in them.

These days usually made me sleepless the night before. Growing up in the country was less eventful and the opportunity for adventure and new toys filled me with excitement. However, that day had a different feel to it than our normal trips to spend time there.

This day felt...unexpected.

When we arrived at my grandmother's apartment, I sat in the living room watching cartoons as I normally did. My parents had left for the hospital and I was left with my grandmother who was in the kitchen at the table in her wheelchair.

My grandmother was a diabetic amputee who had a lot of spice in her veins. She and I never seemed to connect; I was a young boy, and she was an older lady who was almost ashamed to have lost a leg. I know that my grandmother loved me. She attempted to do typical grandmother things with me such as slipping me money behind my parents' backs, saving candy for me, and sticking up for me when

I wanted things that my parents disagreed with. Despite these things, we never seemed to bond closely. Because of that, we were in separate rooms while we were the only two in the apartment.

It was a little before noon when my uncle Marvin walked through the front door to visit with my grandmother. I will never forget his words.

"Bobby passed away."

Some people say that there are key moments in life that put you on a path you were meant to follow. It is very cliché, but at that moment, I felt like I went from being a happy-go-lucky boy to a lost soul.

I had just lost a father figure, a mentor, but more importantly, I had just lost my best friend.

As the tears fell down my cheeks and the world went silent, I thought rapidly and realized how much death is permanent.

Three words kept echoing in my head that day: "Death is final." I am not sure where I had heard those words, but perhaps they came from my inner being or maybe from past experiences of losing pets.

I glanced over at the couch, which was his bed and base of operation, only to realize that he would never see it again. With his things strewn about on the end table, he would no longer pick them up or need them. My mom would never need to pull the television back in the mornings and never again would I hear him arguing with me to turn off the puppets.

No more adventures. No more life lessons. No goodbyes.

My best friend was gone.

4

...BUT NOT A RELATIONSHIP

As I sat in the living room chair, alone and crying, I remember the words that came from my Uncle Marv after he gave the bad news of Bobby's death.

"It appears that his body just couldn't keep up with his drinking," Marv said. "His liver failed, and his body shut down."

It was true. As much as I would like to forever shape him into a legendary hero, Bobby was a drinker—and a heavy one at that. My entire family consists of drinkers and this is how they would gather, with drinks in hand and country songs spilling out of their loose lips.

Bobby's game of cat-and-mouse with alcohol had finally caught up with him, and he was pulled out of the game forever.

Tears streamed down my cheeks, breathing was hard to do, and I sat alone wondering why it had to be the one person who meant the most to me. To most, I am sure Bobby didn't show any value at first glance—he was simple and poor. To me, he meant the world.

At that moment, I found myself making a promise to him that would be secretly kept between us. In honor of his memory, I have vowed to never drink, a promise that I have kept since I was ten years old. It was not easy to keep later on—as any twenty-one-year-old knows—but it was important for me.

After his death, most of my family was pretty tight-lipped when it came to talking about Bobby around me. Many saw him as close to me as my own father, and one of my relatives once said she thought Bobby was my guardian angel. I am not sure if I buy into the whole guardian angels belief, but I do think he was one of those people who comes along so rarely that others must be truly blessed to be able to say that the person was in their lives.

As much as I missed Bobby, I was not the only one. After his death, one of his brothers changed forever as well. Milt, the same brother who had the coin bet with Bobby, worked as a car body repairman and had Bobby's "big blue boat" towed out to his house. Soon thereafter, the vision of the car became too much; being that it was a unique car, he decided to sort it out for parts rather than resell it. He didn't want to meet that particular car on the road again, due to the memories of his young brother.

Even though Bobby is no longer physically here, the memory of our time together and his wisdom still resonate within me. It would be easy to break the promise I made that day, but I won't because it is something that connects me to him. Not a lot of people understand it, but many respect it. It's an oddity to most people I meet, and something I am reluctant to explain the meaning behind because of how personal it is.

I am still surprised I have kept that promise to him after several years but then again, it seems fitting that a man who taught me about promises is remembered by one.

After all, death ends a life, not a relationship.

5

A BELIEF SYSTEM

Each one of us can look back on high school as a time of experimentation with hair, social expression, and fashion. We all have embarrassing moments and triumphs.

My life was no different at Mesabi East High School.

As a teen, I carried a Trapper Keeper to each class and within it, I had various papers such as forms used in conducting a ghost hunt, articles about different cultures, and photos that were a bit "odd," including things labeled as mists, vapors, vortices, orbs, and distorted faces. I would rotate things in and out of the keeper to keep material fresh and interesting.

It was this binder that made high school interesting for me. For each class, I would find a way to relate it to the material I had in the three-ringed binder. Many kids always use the phrase, "When am I ever going to use this?" I was a step ahead of the curve, finding ways to use it in my interests.

Most of my teachers understood my passion for the paranormal. One of the first teachers to recognize this passion was Joseph Legueri.

Mr. Legueri was a teacher I had throughout my high school career in many different subjects. He was a smart and versatile man who had interests in English literature, physical education, and psychology. He was in his late fifties, had a balding head, and thick glasses that would make a Coca Cola bottle fall in love.

When teaching psychology, he agreed to allow freshmen into his class as long as they tested into it. It was an advanced course, and he wanted to know he had a mature class because it went into mature subjects like sexuality and mental disorders as much as a high school can permit.

I sat with him one day before the second semester had started, and we discussed the course of psychology and why I wanted to be involved in it. He had known about my interest in the paranormal and showed me the brief, three-paragraph section in the book about parapsychology.

"Here, take a look at this," he said as he handed me an open textbook. "This is all that you would be taking the course for."

"That's fine," I said. "I want to learn about how the other aspects of psychology affect people's perception of the topics of the paranormal."

He sat back down at his desk and took a moment to react to what I had just said. I had a large lump in my throat. The tension in my mind mounted. I was nervous because I really wanted to take this course!

Then he looked up at me and smiled.

I did end up taking the class and was one of four freshmen to take the course with the upperclassmen that year. It is still one of my favorite classes from high school because it also allowed me to teach for the first time.

When the class reached the parapsychology section of the textbook, Mr. Legueri approached me one day after class and asked if there was anything more I would like to add to the course work.

He gave me the entire next class day to talk to the students about J. B. Rhine, the Spiritualist movement, Uri Geller, and bio-PK feedback. I was thrilled to have the opportunity to speak about the various topics of parapsychology.

As the next school year approached, I entered my sophomore year. Mr. Legueri retired, and I found myself taking a required course for graduation titled "Public Speaking."

The teacher for this class was Mr. Michael Hnatko. He was a larger man with a mustache and beard who always wore a business suit to his classes. He had a deep voice and a certain jolly quality about him. He would always make jokes that made students roll their eyes and could at times be cheesy in his presentation. (However, that is what often made his classes enjoyable.) In a small school, he was another versatile teacher who taught various courses and was breaking ground with this new public speaking course.

Each week, he had us write a speech or presentation with a certain theme. Some examples were how-tos, videos, speeches about a favorite memory, etc. He would always tell us about the theme of the projects as if he were a game show host asking the final *Jeopardy* question, repeating it with a slow, deliberate tone. He wanted us to think deeply about what he wanted us to talk about because he was thrilled to see how creative each student could become.

As the weeks went by, each speech I did involved some aspect of paranormal research. The students were excited about my topics because they were odd and unique. It wasn't the generic "Here is a picture of me and my friends at the lake. It was fun because we all got suntans." I could feel the audience was into the subject material; I would often have to stay after the bell and be late to my next class because I was answering questions!

Mr. Hnatko had no problem with me skewing the course-work to my paranormal interests as it kept him involved in the speeches and created a buzz within the class. The students began to get creative after seeing my presentations, and I found out that I enjoy talking in front of a group of people.

In the next school year, I found myself in another class taught by Mr. Hnatko. One day after class, he approached me to ask a question.

This was another defining moment in my career, because it came at a time when I wanted nothing more than to be normal. I was coming off my sophomore year where it was hard to find a prom date because I spent all my time learning about haunted history. When I did find a date, the person was just embarrassed when the kids had the deejay play the theme song from *Ghostbusters*. When the chorus line of "Who ya gonna call?" came about, they replaced the word "Ghostbusters" with my name.

In short, I was burnt out and longed to be a normal high school student.

"Are you still pursuing your paranormal interests, Adam?" Mr. Hnatko asked me.

"Uhm, yeah ... I think so. Why?" I said with a slight hesitation.

"Well, I was just thinking ..." he said with a pause. "You know for as much as the students in public speaking enjoyed it last year, there must be adults who would enjoy your topics. I know I would love to hear more about it. Have you ever thought of teaching a community education class?"

The truth was that I had never thought of that. I mean, there are a lot of things on a high school student's mind but teaching adults sure isn't one of them.

"No, not really," I said. "How would I even go about doing that?"

6

MARY AND ROY

After my teacher directed me to the right people, I was set to teach a class to adults about my hobby: paranormal research. The local community education office wanted to do something around Halloween time, the only time it was okay to publicly talk about ghosts and spooky things.

For this week in October of 2001, the headline in the community education paper read:

Parapsychology 101—
Ghosts, Hauntings, and the Paranormal:
Come learn about local legends,
what happens after we die, and much more!
Class fee: $5 | Room 203

The curiosity of something so unusual sparked some interest and eventually seven strangers found themselves in a Mesabi East classroom. It contained a mix of men and women ranging from 27 to 52 years of age.

Even after all my travels across the state of Minnesota, I still find myself thinking of this class—I feel very fortunate to have been a part of it. It was as much a learning experience for me as it was for the people who were my students. This class was my first test of many that would come to test social boundaries and break comfort zones of what was taboo to talk about and what could really heal someone's soul.

There was one gentleman who, for the purpose of this story, I will call Roy. He was a slender man in his mid-forties with facial hair in the style of handlebars that was graying. He wore a flannel long-sleeve shirt, common culture in northern Minnesota. Though his clothes gave him a rough appearance, he also wore glasses for reading that seemed to take away from this tough image and show his intellect.

Roy heard about the class from the paper and decided he wanted to broaden his horizons. He'd had many odd experiences in his time and thought the class might provoke a thought that could answer those questions.

Alongside Roy was another student I'll call Mary. She was an older lady who dressed in sweaters that most kids bury in their Christmas gift haul. She had a salt and peppering of gray and brown hair. Like Roy, she also wore glasses, but I believe these were a bit more permanent than Roy's reading spectacles.

Mary heard about the class from a friend who wanted to attend. She decided to give it a shot because, like Roy, she had many questions that needed to be answered. You see, Mary was a widow and had lost her husband about a year ago. She was still very much in the grieving process and wanted some reassurance that her husband was truly in a better place.

For four weeks, we met every Tuesday night at the high school in a classroom. The classes started at 6:00 p.m. and went until 8:00 p.m., but we often ran over the time slot because the conversation and flow of ideas and philosophy were so dynamic. We would find ourselves discussing varied topics from the death process, death in literature, how paranormal investigating equipment worked, and why each of us was in the classroom.

To me, Roy was the moral support that helped me get through the classes. He was the one who kept cheering me on and giving me feedback on each night's lesson. He was always on the edge of his seat, it seemed. Each night, he would come up to me and pat me on the back, smile, and say, "See you next week. Great job!"

One night, the class was discussing the differences in ghosts and how the paranormal field classifies different cases based on the activity experienced. We talked about the three types of hauntings, including residual (a tape loop effect of an event), traditional (an intelligent and interactive haunting), and a crisis apparition.

The last type usually occurs when someone has recently passed. These revolve around a "crisis" event such as a death and are usually reported within a time frame of anywhere from an hour before death to seventy-two hours after death. The goal of this type of communication from the dead to the living is to help the living grieve and get past whatever is troubling them, usually the loss of their loved one.

The rest of the class went on without much of a disturbance; I drew diagrams and notes, and explained crisis apparition examples with the class. When the class ended, most of them left and Roy did his usual pat on my back and said, "Good job."

Mary, however, stuck around. In all the classes I have spoken to, I have found this to be a common occurrence: people like to keep things private, in fear of society's gaze. After all, no one wants to be perceived as crazy.

She approached me as I began to pack up my materials.

"Can I talk to you?" she asked while fidgeting with her fingers nervously.

"Certainly. What's going on?" I responded.

"Well, I really enjoyed the class tonight, but it brought up some questions for me. I lost my husband about a year ago, and it has been a hard time without him. I heard what you said about the crisis apparitions and I never knew that is what it was called," Mary explained. "He passed away last June, and about a week after his death, I was in the bedroom, getting things of his packed away. I began to cry because I missed him so much."

Mary began to tear up and her speech got a bit shaky, but she tried to push through her experience so she could share it with me.

"I thought I heard him come into our bedroom, and I felt as if he was there with me. I stopped crying then. I do not know what it was, and I brushed it off. The next day, I was coming home from a relative's house. We have this large Christmas star on our garage and I noticed that it was lit up. I don't like to have things on while I am gone in fear of fire, so I went to go unplug it. I found out that it was not plugged in. I went to go look to see if it was still on and it was, but suddenly turned off when I was staring at it. It spooked me."

I was now leaning against a desk as this lady poured her heart out to me. I didn't have to listen to her story, but I am glad I did.

"I sat here and listened to your story about crisis apparitions and thought to myself about that night the star lit up. There was no reason for it to come on, but I had forgotten that it was my husband's pride and joy to hang that up every year. When he passed, I didn't have the heart to take it down," Mary said with tears running down her face.

Then she dropped the hardest question I've ever faced.

"Do you think it was him that night trying to contact me to say 'I am all right'?"

I gave myself a few minutes to take that all in and rationalize an answer. This was not easy, because my answer would either give her relief and comfort or be as cold as a long Minnesota winter. Without knowing or seeing the event myself, I had no perspective on it but had to answer.

So I did.

"It very well could have been," I said with a slight uneasy smile afterwards.

"That's all that I needed to hear! Thank you so much," Mary cried out as she reached out to hug me.

I honestly do not know if it was her husband reaching out to comfort her, but sometimes the answers are not as easy as a yes or no. My conversation with Mary would be one of my first lessons in rights and responsibilities. It comes with the territory, and is something that many within the so-called "paranormal community" have yet to realize as they charge for events that exploit the dead, pretend to be psychics who have the answers from loved ones for book deals, and those who march around haunted locations like they run the show (and *are* often on television shows).

To this day, I still think about both Mary and Roy. I was fortunate to have these two people on my journey as guides; they taught me about gratitude and being earnest.

I learned that if you take time out for others, you will be rewarded in some way. It may not be money; money can leave but the memory of these two will never leave.

7

NEW HORIZONS

After I graduated from high school in 2003, I wanted to leave the area I called home. I wanted to explore the bigger urban areas. I think it's a rite of passage for people to want to explore the world around them.

After much searching through high school, I found my destination in the town of Mankato. It was a town located five hours south of the Iron Range with a population of around 40,000 people. It was a booming college town that held the NFL training camp for the Minnesota Vikings, about an hour south of the Twin Cities. I was still able to venture into "the Cities" for a day if I needed to find some adventure, but I was able to relax in a much smaller fishbowl.

When I moved to Mankato, I was surprised at how much more there was to this town than what I was used to. The biggest surprise to me, however, was the difference in cultural history from my home town.

The Mankato area was much older and more vital to the history of Minnesota's early statehood. There were many important Mankato area citizens who served in the Civil War, the Sioux Uprising of 1862, and many who helped put Minnesota on the map as a worldly location. Some of these figures included the Mayo Brothers, who went on to found the world-famous Mayo Clinic, and General Ramsey, who eventually went on to become the state's first governor.

However, being new to the area at the time, I didn't know Madison Avenue from Victory Drive—I had a lot of legwork to do so I could understand my new home. My first steps were taken at the local college campus as an incoming freshman with a passion for things that went bump in the night. I began asking what the "spooky tales" were in the area, and many students were happy to talk about them. Now that I had the locations, I just needed some local help to explore these areas.

In 2005, I began searching for the staff that would be the first formal MNPSG team. As one can imagine, it is not easy to find others who are as interested in history and tragic stories of lost souls pre-paranormal entertainment boom. At the time, your best chance to watch a paranormal show was *Buffy the Vampire Slayer*.

So how does one reach out to the public to uncover these select people?

I decided to reach out to whoever read my website at the time, called "ParaStudy." It was nothing like MinnesotaGhosts.com is today, and amazingly, I found people who read it. Oddly enough, people responded to the staff ad on it!

Finding new people who fit into your vision can be a tough thing to do. Each person has to be a perfect fit. To this day, I am still really exclusive with the people I choose to be part of my team, which a lot of people don't understand. I have turned down friends and family for application within my team, which makes for some awkward situations.

However, there is a reason I am so picky when it comes to new members. It takes a certain person to become a ghost hunter. It's not always black GMCs and walkie-talkies. It is not an easy lifestyle, and it is easily misunderstood. I have lived like this for years, and it is hard for most people to see the excitement the television shows portray.

A ghost hunter needs to care about people, be passionate and almost entrepreneurial in their approach, okay with being up at four in the morning, smart, communicative, honest, good with kids, of the highest integrity, tech savvy, brave, humorous, determined, and creative.

Each person I have worked with has shown me these abilities in one way or another. I must be honest in saying that these traits have also taken people away from my team. The only consolation is that I was lucky enough to work with these people at the peak of their passion for the paranormal.

This is a completely new field, and the advances come from people who exhibit all these abilities. The people who creep around in the dark looking for an answer that may not even exist are true pioneers. I am not willing to take on people who can't check for spelling errors in emails, lack respect, or just want to tag along because it would be "cool." That doesn't cut it for me. You have to bring something to the table in order to sit for dinner.

To help me weed out some of the people I thought would not be a good fit, I employed a simple trick in my application process. Below the paragraph of legal mumbo jumbo, I typed the word "BLUE" into a box. When an application came through my email inbox, I only had to look to see if this person was the type to pay attention to details. It was quite funny to see the responses people put into this blank box when all they had to do was read what was in front of them. After all, I wanted people who wouldn't let little things pass them by in investigations.

Humans are amazing creatures, and I am fortunate to be able to have my life's story interlaced with so many great people. After all, Dorothy's tale wouldn't be much without her friends.

8

A SAFETY MEASURE

One thing I admire in people is a sense of determination. I was lucky enough to have met one person named Kelly who defined the word "determined."

When I originally put out a call for team members for the group via the ParaStudy website, Kelly was one of those people who had sent a letter of inquiry to me about joining the team.

Unfortunately, she was the only one who met my strict requirements at the time. Since she was the only applicant, I never took a chance at that time to start the group. My goal was to truly break in a group of people rather than just one applicant. I had filed Kelly's email away but never forgotten about her.

Almost a year later, I had finally found what I considered to be the group of people I was looking for. I had set up a meeting for the first five members of the MNPSG crew to meet up at the local library for a meeting in a conference room. However, I wanted to get to know this determined member and take her on an early ghost hunt as a way to say, "Thanks for waiting for a year and never giving up on me."

I decided to check out a local cemetery with a good friend of mine and asked Kelly to join us. We were going to meet up at a rural cemetery around 11 p.m. and her husband had reservations when she made mention of her scheduled plans, and for good reason.

"You're going to do what?!" he asked. "Well, if you are so nuts to go off to do this, take your sister with you." (Why he chose to sacrifice his sister-in-law if things were to go wrong was beyond me!) At any rate, Kelly invited her sister to join.

As we pulled up to the cemetery, we found Kelly and her sister talking to a local police officer who was interested in why two young women were at a cemetery so late at night. He had no problem with us being there but was just doing a service to make sure that everything was "right."

Once we got there, the police officer left and Kelly shared her husband's concern with us.

I laughed about the situation because often times I find myself thinking very differently than most when it comes to this type of situation. This is not an unusual lifestyle for me, but to others I often forget it is. I have gone on numerous investigations with friends and spent so much time in cemeteries at night that I failed to see the concern. It was good to hear that Kelly's husband had put this situation into perspective for our team!

Kelly ended up being an instrumental member of the foundation of the early group. She provided a professional quality to our group with a hint of childlike curiosity that ignited a spark within our team. She eventually left our team due to a move out of state. I often miss her for the ambition she showed in our early adventures.

9

A FOUNDATION BUILDS STRENGTH

Shortly after meeting Kelly at that rural cemetery, the team held a meeting at the Blue Earth County Public Library. The original team had five members from all backgrounds. I had purposely picked each member from a pool of applicants for both personal and professional traits. The team consisted of myself, Kelly, Monica, Nancy, and Kurt.

Kelly was a 29-year-old mother who worked as a photo researcher for a publishing company in southern Minnesota. She always seemed to be bright, cheery, and brave. I chose this applicant because she was someone who knew how to dig deep for answers on projects. When you need historical information, it is an invaluable asset to have someone with an ambitious drive.

The second person was a customer service representative by day named Monica. She was also a 29-year-old mother, and she loved cross-stitching and rock and roll music. I chose Monica because she was down to earth, took no BS, yet was polite enough to complete strangers, as she was in customer service. When you are working with people who claim to have haunted stories, it doesn't matter what you personally think—it's real to them. That means sometimes you have to grin and bear it but also know enough to separate fact from fiction. This kind of skill lets you know where to start in investigating claims. I knew Monica brought this quality to the team.

The third lady that was chosen to be on this new team was a 52-year-old named Nancy. In her application, she told me about all her hopes and desires to make paranormal conventions, her love of books about ghosts, and her willingness to help drive the team around in her van. She was passionate about finding ghosts, which is something I have found out is a very important quality to have in a team. You need that spark to light a fire when times get tough. Her intensity for investigations inspired us all.

And my final piece of the team was Kurt, who was from the Twin Cities area where he served as a police officer. I can't say much else for him, as he never made it to the meeting for reasons I will never know. I chose him for the obvious honesty of being a law enforcement officer but in the end, he served as an example that people can sometimes lose focus in their endeavors. Sometimes that fire inside burns out or we realize we don't have the time at that moment to pursue certain dreams.

For the rest of that afternoon, I discussed my expectations with my new friends. I was giving them an opportunity to do something that can at times make you feel as though you've slipped down a rabbit hole and into a magical world. When you truly experience a haunted location with bizarre activity, it is easy for logic to take a back seat.

I always thought I was teaching them about ghost hunting, but over the course of our adventures, they would teach me in many ways about various qualities of life. I look fondly back on that afternoon, because it was the start of something wonderful.

This first meeting laid down the foundation of the Minnesota Paranormal Study Group. It was people, and it still is people.

10

INVESTIGATING 101

Over the many years I have been involved with investigating the paranormal, I've created a formula for conducting business. These methods have evolved over the years, and I have had the ability to try a variety of different equipment.

The first step to a formal investigation is to find a suitable case. I receive case leads from emails and by word of mouth by the cartload each month, but only a few are suitable for my team. Various factors are taken into consideration such as scheduling, travel, what the case involves for activity, and whether we would be able to properly document it. The last one is the most important, because if you aren't able to document the activity, what are you providing the client other than using them for your hope to get scared in the dark? If the location allows us to experience a bit of history, we might take it; even if we are unable to capture anything paranormal, we can always document and share the historical stories the property holds.

When we arrive at a location, we ask that a staff member or the property owner give us a tour of the location and share the stories with us. While doing this, we keep our cameras rolling so we can document their stories as well as capture any odd experience that happens while we are on tour. Activity happens a lot when we are receiving a tour, and we have learned to record during this time after missing some experiences.

When the tour is over, we determine the "hot spots" of activity. These are the locations where we will place equipment and send teams to investigate. During this time, we break into groups of three people or smaller. We have found out that if you have a group larger than three, activity is less likely to happen—the unknown seems to get stage fright!

We then begin to investigate by doing electronic voice phenomena (EVP), asking open-ended questions out loud while recording audio, as well as filming video. We also use devices such as electromagnetic field (EMF) meters (which is sometimes called the Cell Sensor), K2 meters (record a specific range of electromagnetic field), and the Mel Meter (measures temperature, EMF, and K2 frequencies). These allow us to get an environmental read on the location and sometimes allow us the chance to communicate with the spirits.

On certain investigations, we use special equipment such as the infrared strobe, laser grid, and shack hack. These devices are used rarely in our investigation because they are still in the experimental phase.

After our investigations, we research any needed historical data and review all of our data including audio and video. This is then condensed into a video format documenting our investigation and given to the client via a personal DVD or through an email link depending on travel and scheduling. We consult with the client and answer any questions that they have before we release the information to the public via our website.

This is the standard process we use time and time again for the remainder of this book, and I feel it is important to state it here rather than repeat it several times in the stories that follow.

PART TWO

11

THE LE SUEUR COUNTY HISTORICAL MUSEUM

During my time in southern Minnesota, one of my favorite investigation locales came to be the Le Sueur County Historical Society Museum. (It goes by a different name these days, due to a different organization that owns and operates it.)

In the small town of Elysian, Minnesota, is a small red brick building on a hill. The three-level building was originally used as the Elysian Public School in 1895. The building housed students of the area until 1963; however, not a single student graduated from the institution. Those who did graduate from the area were sent to another nearby school.

In 1965, the building was bought by the county historical society for $14.50. The building at this time was discussed as possibly being torn down after sitting dormant for two years, as it no longer served a purpose. At a city meeting, the historical society proposed that it could be used as a museum. After a heated debate, a local stood up and cried out, "Here, just buy it for them already!" and pulled out the cash he had in his pocket: $14.50.

After two years remodeling it into a museum, it was officially opened as the Le Sueur County Historical Museum.

I originally learned about this museum from my good friend and mentor, John Savage of the Minnesota Paranormal Investigators Group (MNPIG). It was in August of 2005 that John and the MNPIG organization invited my team to do a joint investigation with them. This was my first time being able to investigate with John and his team despite many phone calls and email questions. Investigating with another team is a wonderful way to learn from each other in methods and practices. Since the MNPIG team operates from a psychical approach, it was interesting for my scientific team to witness their investigating techniques.

This was going to be my first investigation with the three founding members of the team, so we had a lot to learn as a group. I was also able to get some insight on the new members. Kelly, Monica, Nancy, and I carpooled from Mankato to nearby Elysian, and we all were excited for this opportunity.

We arrived at the museum at dusk. Most of John's team was outside waiting for nightfall. After a few brief hellos, John and I entered the museum where he introduced me to the caretaker at the time, Nancy Burhop. She was a small lady with glasses, and reminded me of a librarian.

Since John's team was waiting on the dark of night, I asked Nancy to take my team on a tour of the location and explain to me why she had invited a paranormal research team to investigate. This gave my team the chance to focus on the hot spots of previous activity and also separate our team from the MNPIG, who did not wish to know the previous activity or history due to their psychic approach. Nancy was more than happy to give us the tour.

For being in a small building, this museum packed quite a bit within its variety of rooms and exhibits.

The main floor consisted of a lobby, a beautiful red staircase, the public bathrooms, a display room of an old general store, and three rooms modeled in the late 1890s: a bedroom, kitchen, and sitting room. These rooms were roped off to prevent visitors from touching the artifacts.

The second floor had the main offices for the staff, a school room setting, the Hall of Memories, a room dedicated to one donor's miniature shoe collection, and a religious room that included old robes and sacred garb from the area's churches—including a confessional booth! The Hall of Memories was a long wooden hallway with several armed forces and occupational displays behind glass.

Nancy claims to have heard unexplainable noises coming from the museum during her time working there. One such story depicts when she and another museum volunteer were working on the museum newsletter and heard the hand bell outside the upstairs office door. When they opened the door, they were startled to see that there was no one in the museum and the hand bell was sitting where it had been left, on the ground-level reception desk.

One day, a volunteer entered the museum and heard the giggling of a small child coming from the grand red staircase. When she went upstairs to ask Nancy if she had her granddaughter with her for the day, she was surprised to find out that not a single child had been in the building all day.

The ground-level bathroom has its own story behind it as well. Many who enter to use the restroom always will be a little uneasy after one young girl had a run-in with a mischievous spirit. A young girl was listening to the stories of the museum's supernatural inhabitants and thought it would be appropriate to stick out her tongue to mock the spirits. Later, she entered the restroom and as she tried to leave, the door was held shut by an unseen force. The young lady described it as if someone was playing tug of war on the other end with her. After many attempts to pull the door open, the girl stopped for a while and when she tried again, the door opened without a problem.

While talking to a few visitors in the lobby, Nancy had heard large crashing noises coming from the basement. She was afraid that other guests were breaking museum pieces, so she rushed down there to investigate. When she asked the guests in the basement what they were doing and explained the noises she had heard, the visitors were just as confused. They too had heard the noises but thought they were coming from the ground-level floor above them.

In the room called the 1900 Room sits an old Edison phonograph. One day, Nancy was cleaning a nearby artifact room when she heard music playing out of the old phonograph. She was baffled—she knew a pencil was stuck in there that would prevent the needle from touching the cylinder. When she reached the phonograph, she saw that nothing was moving and the pencil was still in its place. However, the music still echoed from the machine. Startled and scared, Nancy left that room with haste.

The 1900 Room also has a barrel with dominos set on it. A psychic who previously visited had pointed out the dominos as a very loud distraction during his time at the museum. He claimed that the black game·pieces were constantly clacking together and drawing his attention away from what he was trying to perceive. Curious, Nancy did a test with white cleaning powder and set up the dominos. After a week of having this powder on the top of the barrel, she noticed that the dominos moved a bit in the powder.

One of the strangest parts of the museum has to be in the basement area. This area is used for storage and has three display rooms: a tool room, a loom room, and a jug room.

In the tool room is a male entity who is said to rush up in the face of visitors. This of course startles those who come face to face with the man. This entity also has removed all the wooden planes off the peg board wall and laid them out for Nancy to pick up. When she saw this, she got irritated by the spirit's hijinks and gave him an earful.

Various other objects have been moved out of place in this room, such as a pair of large black mittens that usually are on a red sled.

The loom room has its fair share of spirits as well. Many visitors have reported seeing apparitions of small children in the room. On several encounters, visitors have reported feeling being pushed in the back by an unseen force while facing the support pole in the room.

During one tour, Nancy had been explaining to the public tour that the loom room had been reported to have a lot of paranormal activity by a psychic. While she was talking about what the psychic said, she noticed the group was looking at something over her shoulder. When she turned around, she noticed the door behind her was swinging on its own.

To have this much reported activity in a building the size of this museum was unheard of, but how much of it was real and what was over-imagination? It was my team's job to document and separate fact from fiction.

After the tour, we joined back up with John's MNPIG members who were exploring the outer perimeter of the property.

We began our investigation by a walkthrough with John's crew to see what they had psychically discovered. They found these things psychically by walking the location with their hands outstretched and often eyes closed. They mentioned there were some kids in the museum who liked to run up and down the main staircase. John was also pretty adamant about encountering a man who was mean to him in the basement near the tool room who John claimed would "be going rounds with him later on in the night."

As a team, we decided this investigation would be spent observing John's team to see what we could learn while our equipment did most of the documentation work. Observing MNPIG would let us make sure no psychic shenanigans were taking place, as this investigation style seemed odd to us.

It was John's decision that the teams would gather in the basement to do a channeling session. I figured that I would be up for observing this while trying to verify their claims with my equipment. This activity intrigued me, as it is something I read about a lot in my research but never had the chance to see in application.

Some may think me a bit odd for having a skewed perspective; I am skeptical of psychical research but am involved in a field full of stories about full-bodied apparitions, objects moving on their own, and entities that we call ghosts. For many, these two fields fall into the same category—the paranormal. My view on these two fields show an overlap where I think psychics can be an asset to helping in investigations because, let's face it, we don't know everything about an unknown field. I am willing to try out different approaches. My core beliefs are based in science and being able to show some documented data for an objective control. In order for an investigation to be considered successful, I need data that is not influenced by someone's personal feelings. This data can be a video segment of an apparition, audio recorder of a clear EVP, or even sometimes historical information. Psychical stories are strictly subjective and personal to a specific person.

In a channeling session, a psychic medium sits within a group of people and invites a spirit to enter the body of the medium and interact with the group. John had pulled up a wooden chair and put his back to the group so he could concentrate.

Being new to this type of activity, I was skeptical about the channeling session but at the same time, I wanted to see how different approaches could possibly yield results. While trying to concentrate, John explained that he was using his third eye to watch the room and asked if I would take baseline readings in a corner of the tool room. I agreed because it gave me a chance to document something free from human contamination.

When I reached the spot of the basement he wanted me to probe with my EMF meter, I had a very startling experience. I felt a sudden weight on my shoulders as if someone ran up behind me and tried to leap over me like in a failed game of leap frog. This was followed by a suffocating feeling I can only relate to swimming. Do you know the experience when you are underwater and panic because you are out of air but still have a long ways to go to the surface? Yeah, that was the feeling!

I passed off my EMF meter to Monica and excused myself to go outside to regain my composure. The experience was very startling, and I needed some time to catch my breath. I also wanted some time to figure out what exactly transpired in that room and how John guided me to that location with that effect happening shortly after his instructions.

Once I had enough time to catch my breath, I rejoined others in the basement where John was talking in a different tone of voice. He had made mention of me when I was coming down the stairs and mentioned that I shouldn't have gotten in his space.

The tone John was now speaking in was a deeper, slower, and more serious tone than he had been using when we first arrived. I have spent many hours with him talking on the phone, and this was unlike anything I had ever heard. He had gone from the personality of a carefree standup comedian to John Wayne. I wasn't entirely sure that this entity was speaking through John and whether he was successfully channeling, especially since I left the room for a prolonged amount of time despite my team witnessing the whole session. I wasn't sure if I completely believed it, but I had no explanation for whatever attacked me on a very personal level.

The entity had made mention that his name was Willie and that he was once the caretaker of the school that was in this building. It was his job to care for the building, and he didn't care for Nancy's antics in "his" building.

"I am the caretaker now, Willie!" she said with an irritated tone. "Are you the one who took the tools off the wall?"

"Yes, I didn't like them that way," Willie said through John.

"Do you remember what I said to you that day?" Nancy asked.

In a very evil and deep voice through John came Willie's reply; "Yeah ... (laughs) ... you were pretty angry." A smile came over his face in a slow and maniacal fashion. "That's why I slammed the toilet seat."

Despite the inability to get any concrete data to prove that the channeling was a success, the MNPIG team had a map drawn for Nancy of how Willie wanted the tools on the wall to be arranged. She later switched what was asked to be changed and never had another problem in the tool room.

After the channeling session, John and I had decided to go do some EVPs on the third floor near the school room with a digital audio recorder. (I was still wondering about John's change of vocal tone as he seemed to be back to normal now. Logically, it didn't add up.) We stood at the end of the Hall of Memories with John asking questions about who was there, what they were doing there, and other typical EVP recording questions. After a few minutes, he would rush back to his laptop and try to listen to what was recorded.

On one recording, we heard a very distinct voice echo out of the darkness, "Just give it up!"

John took offense to this and got upset. He rushed back into the school room and said, "Whoever told us to just give it up, we are not going to do that!" He then went on with a long conversation with his recorder running about why we were there. I can't remember the rest because I felt a small tug on the right pant leg of my shorts. Out of instinct, I looked down.

I saw a small boy in a blue tint with his hands on my shorts. He looked like he had been in a swimming pool too long; his lips were tinted blue and there was darkness under his eyes. The boy appeared to be about eight or nine years old and was dressed in a tweed coat. We seemed to make eye contact for an eternity but in all reality, it was probably only three seconds.

He looked into my eyes and asked, "Can you help us then?"

I was baffled beyond comprehension as I tried to reach over to my left and slap John on the shoulder. After waving my hand in the air for a while, I looked at John and grabbed his shirt but when I looked back down, the boy was gone.

I asked to go listen to the recorder. I didn't want to tell him what I had just heard from the little boy but did mention to John that I saw him.

On John's recorder, you could hear the small boy say, "Can you help us then?"

I was so emotionally shaken at this point that I did not know what to do. My brain told me to leave the building, but my heart told me to stay. I was uneasy to go into that school room in the pitch black again because I had just come face to face with a ghost child. It hit me so emotionally that my eyes started to fill with tears and my body's natural response was to start shaking. I was not reacting very well physically, but mentally I was thrilled!

I have seen or heard ghosts on other occasions. In cases following this, I heard EVP files with my name called out, I have seen ghosts run away from me (which we will talk about later), and have felt phantom finger tips on my back in a number of investigations. However, I have never had a direct and personal confrontation with a ghost before. This touched me, spoke to me, and let me see it. Hell, it made eye contact with me! My brain wanted me to explain it away but it knew that all three senses could not lie like that. Not to mention that we now had it on the recorder! The experience was as real as real could have ever been.

The team wanted to try to record more EVP in the school room as a group after they heard about John and I having success. We invited Nancy Burhop to join us up there and while sitting in the pitch black, I felt her grab my arm and hold on tight. This was a charming moment of the night, as I had a stranger grab my arm for comfort. To me, this was the type of action that defines the investigator/client relationship and why many do this without pay. Nancy was on edge—and for good reason.

As the night burned through darkness, my body eventually calmed down and the experiences there helped fuel my curiosity to investigate more cases. It was around 2 a.m. when all activity ceased and even our weather equipment registered data; a drop in barometric pressure, the temperature rose, and the humidity decreased.

We decided to call it a night and head back to our beds so that we could review the evidence and wrap our heads around the night's experiences. Unfortunately, we did not find much more concrete evidence for our experiences other than John's EVP audio files from that night.

There is no doubt in my mind that there is something at the Le Sueur County Historical Society Museum. Over the next few years, I took the time to visit Nancy Burhop at the museum and see what the ghosts were up to. They always seemed to make their presence known whenever I visited.

My first trip back to the museum was about a year after our initial investigation. Nancy had since gained complete control of the museum. Whenever something unusual happened, she would bark out an order and put the spirits in their place. I thought it was so cool that her personality had changed from our initial meeting; she had gone from meek to responsible. Seeing this change in clients is a true reward for all the long nights. I like to think that our work gives these people the ability to be comfortable in their own homes and work environments. Nancy was now empowered and no longer afraid.

During this visit, Nancy was showing me around the third floor and telling me about recent experiences she'd had. We found out that the lights would not turn on in the school room. Upset, Nancy demanded that the spirits turn on the lights by the next time she was upstairs.

After concluding our tour in the basement, we decided to talk in her office on the third floor. On the walk up the stairs, I noticed that the light in the school room was on. I paused a bit and walked down the Hall of Memories saying, "No way…" I checked the light switch and it was now in the "on" position, and no one had been around to turn it on.

Sure enough, the lights were on in the school room. The person who had come along with me on this trip was in disbelief as well. I said thank you out loud to whoever turned on the light, and as we walked out of the room, we heard the sound of a book slamming against the floor. We both spun around and went to explore the noise we'd just heard and found nothing out of order.

In those situations, it's best to just crack a smile and shake your head. This field is so full of surprises, and they don't all need explanations.

12

THE SADDLE HOME

The Saddle Family was perfectly normal at first glance. Marie was a single mother who worked at a call center for a national company and had three children. Her oldest was a boy named Henry who just had turned thirteen and was into sports of all kinds. She also had two daughters. Maebelle was the middle child who had just turned ten years old, and Samantha was the youngest at age eight.

The family had lived on a popular lake next to a ski resort in southern Minnesota. The land was originally used by the local Native American tribe as a settlement in the 1860s. In fact, the lake was even named after the local tribe. The split-level home the Saddles lived in was fairly modern and still smelled like construction materials and fresh paint. It had a remarkable view of the lake and was more than anyone needed and everything one could want in a home.

In February of 2006, I heard about the Saddle family through a friend who worked with Marie. He knew I was into the paranormal and passed along her information to me one night. Monica, my case manager, contacted her, and we set up an investigation for the following weekend.

The night before we were set to do our investigation, I had a very striking and terrible dream. In this dream, I was walking up to a white house with a wraparound porch and a white front door that had a circle of glass on it. As I walked up to the home, I noticed that the front door was open. Once I set foot on the front step, I felt as if I were being pulled off the porch from behind. As this was happening, the front door slammed shut. I then woke up, shaken. I sat in my bed for a few moments and wondered what it all meant. It's said that when dreams stay with you, it is a sign that they contain information from the other side. Was this the case?

The next day, I called my colleague and good friend John Savage (mentioned earlier in this book). I described my dream to him, and he said he was getting the feeling that whatever was there was afraid of me entering the home. As obvious as this was, he also mentioned that an older male spirit had been there for a long time. He advised me to be cautious about this gentleman.

As much as I trusted John, I took his advice with a grain of salt; it was just too general for my liking. As stated prior, I am more of the type who needs objective evidence despite various odd situations I have encountered in my life. You don't always get clear solutions for the situations that make you scratch your head, and this was certainly one of them.

The team that night consisted of Monica, Nancy, Kelly, and myself. Much to my horror, the house was the exact house from my dream! It was a white split-level home with a wraparound porch on it. There was a garage and driveway off to the right of the porch area. Suddenly, I was thrust back into my dream as I started to walk cautiously to the front door. I expected to be pulled back as I stepped on the porch like in my dream, but I made it into the home just fine without any odd activity. I realized how foolishly I let my mind and emotions wander back into the dream.

We met with Marie, and she told us the children were with her ex-husband. I was absolutely amazed at the beauty of this home and the layout. If I were to build a home of my dreams, I could not expect it to be any less than this!

Marie must have picked up on my adoration for the home. She asked if we wanted a tour and hear the stories that brought us there. I told her that we did but I wanted to walk around for a few minutes to get my bearings. I walked around and picked up on a few different feelings.

(This was my experimental phase of research on sensitivity to paranormal activity and a psychical approach. John's group and their results from the museum investigation had me curious.)

My first stop on my walkthrough was in Henry's room in the basement level of the home. Nancy followed me, taking notes of whatever I talked about. I mentioned that something liked to be in this room and that the closet was where it had been hiding. It was a very odd feeling being in that room; it felt very voyeuristic to me. Worse, I knew it was a child's bedroom, a fact I found disturbing.

The next stop was in Samantha's room down the hall. When we entered, I asked Nancy to turn out the light. She did so as I put my head in the closet and felt something hiding in here as well. I backed out of the closet and stood next to the bed. I asked whatever was in there to come out and show itself. Much to my surprise, the gray figure of a little girl emerged. She was as solid as one would expect a human to be except she seemed to be blurry, translucent, and black and white. She had light colored hair, a white dress with a sash in the middle, and she wore black patent-leather shoes. She went to go sit down on the floor and seemed to lose her footing. She plopped down on her butt and looked at me. It appeared she was rolling a toy along the floor. I could not see the toy, but she kept looking at me as if to say, "Do you want to play?" even though her lips never moved.

I continued to try communicating with her, asking questions that would help us out such as "What is your name? Did you die here? Are you scared?" The child didn't seem to care about any of these questions and kept playing. At some point, she must have realized that I did not care to play with her and started to fade away. After she disappeared, I had my first lesson of the night: talk about what *they* want to talk about.

We walked out of the room and my mind was racing. I'd never had that type of interaction where a spirit had completely stood me up because I didn't want to play with them. It was humorous and enlightening. Being scientific-minded, sometimes one loses focus of the humanity in the things we study. Just like real kids act in front of a doctor who asks too many boring questions, you will lose these spirits' attention if you can't get on their level.

We checked out Maebelle's room but did not find any oddities. We started to walk towards Henry's room again when I noticed the feeling of an older man following us. I had made mention of this to Nancy and said that his name was either "Ralph" or "Charlie." I am not sure where these names came from other than just popping into my head. He was an older gentleman who appeared to be like Fred Gwynne's character in *Pet Sematary*. He was tall, simple, had gray hair, and was wearing overalls. He appeared to be a farmer. My closest way of identifying him as a farmer was my friend's dad, Charlie, who was also a farmer. (In hindsight, this is most likely why the name Charlie came into my head; something was reminding me of him!) I had told him that we were not there to disturb anything but wanted to help the family. He backed off a bit, but it felt as if he was watching us like a store clerk watches a group of teenagers; he didn't want any funny business and wanted to make sure we didn't take anything.

We then regrouped with Marie and the other investigators in the upstairs living room. I had just sat down on the couch to tell Marie my stories about the basement level when suddenly I felt drawn to the fireplace. I asked her what it was made of, and she replied that it was made out of an old pipe organ. I told her that I felt as if someone would stand in front of this and be very proud of the craftsmanship. She said that nothing had ever happened around that particular fireplace that she knew of. I told her that it was odd because there was such an interesting feeling around it, but I brushed it off and sat back down on the couch.

Telling her of my experience in Henry's room, I could see she was a bit shaken. Since my case manager handled this case and the background, I knew very little of the actual reports of activity, which was how I wanted to keep it so I could test my psychical research approach. Marie became a bit distressed after my story and told us what happened in Henry's room.

"My son, who is thirteen, claims to see a shadow figure come out of his closet and sit on the edge of his bed at night. He can't sleep, and I feel so helpless. He said he has even tried kicking at it to scare it away, which usually works. The thing that really scares him is that one night he had kicked it and said that he hit something solid…and it did not go away," Marie explained.

"He also brings down those large fast-food cups, you know like the 44 oz. ones, which he fills with water so he doesn't have to come upstairs to the kitchen at night. He doesn't drink that much water, but in the morning, the cups are empty—there is not even a drop of water left. They are completely dry. That is kind of scary to both of us. Have you ever encountered something like that before?"

I shook my head, now very interested in her story. At the time, this was new territory for me and my team. Since this case, I have found shadow figures to be kind of pervasive beings that hover around young children. This was one of the first cases where I would run into a shadow figure that haunted a child; since then, I have worked on other cases where the symptoms of a shadow person are consistent with this one. Typically, shadow figures are found in areas children frequent at night, involve consuming a form of water, and seem to watch kids for whatever reason. Some have even reported seeing shadow people that have red eyes. Many investigators don't know what these entities are. Are they human? Something else? Are they another form of life coming from a parallel dimension? They have a curious nature, and never seem to do any harm other than scare or startle those they visit.

I told Marie about my encounter with the ghost girl in Samantha's room, and much to my surprise, Marie started crying. Monica, who was sitting next to her, wrapped her arm over Marie's shoulder. I sat there with my head down and waited for the truth of Samantha's room to come out when Marie was ready.

"This house used to be owned by my uncle and aunt. We had bought it from them when they decided to move a few years ago. Since then, we have remodeled the home quite extensively. I loved this house, and I used to stay here as a child. The guest room I stayed in is now Samantha's room. One night when I was down there, I heard something come from the closet and felt as if something crawled into bed with me. I didn't know what it was at the time, as the heating vents were noisy. The house was strange to me," Marie confessed.

"Recently, I was in Sam's room sorting her laundry. I was in front of the closet and folding her clothes, getting them ready to put in her dresser. I sat on the end of her bed and heard a noise coming from the closet, as if someone was moving around in there. The doors were moving so I thought it was Sam playing hide and seek with me. She knew I was going to be doing her laundry so I started to say, 'Oh geez, I wonder who is in the closet! I'm going to get you!' I put my hands on the knobs of the accordion door for the closet and yanked it open as fast as I could. There was no one in there, and the noises stopped.

"I knew that Samantha could not have gotten out of there without me seeing her, so I went upstairs and asked the kids if they were making noises. I was shaken up and nervous, so I yelled at them. I regret it, but it happened."

My team sat there in disbelief. I was now in tears myself, shocked and concerned about the fact that the girl I had seen was not just something in my imagination! She was reported and real. How could I have known this? Was it what I experienced? More importantly, was I really stood up by a ghostly toddler?! You always want to second-guess your own personal experiences, but this one was now just confirmed by a complete stranger who had her own run-in with the entity.

Marie explained that she was now quite frightened in her own home. She was looking into selling it and moving in with her boyfriend, Mike, a deputy with the sheriff's department. She also went on to explain that she still experiences the feeling of something crawling into bed with her at night. Oddly, this happened in their bedroom, which is on a different floor from her daughter's room where she had experienced it as a young girl. An unseen person crawling into their bedroom was so real that even Mike had experienced it.

I told her then about the farmer gentleman and his approach to watching us. I asked her if she knew of a "Charlie" or "Ralph." Maybe it was a relative; the house had been in the family for a while now. She said she did not know who it could have been, so we left it at that. You can't win them all.

Marie shared some photos from around the home she believed had some oddities. She showed us a photo of a mirror that appears to have someone standing in it with eyes all around it. She mentioned seeing a wolf-like creature in it, and I explained "matrixing" to her.

Matrixing is when the human mind begins to recognize familiar patterns in chaotic patterns. You might start to see faces in tree bark or recognize a cloud as an animal. This phenomenon happens often in the paranormal field, and I usually overlook photos where people report to see faces in ghostly pictures because of it.

Marie confessed that what really messed with the family was the sound of hearing their names called by other family members during daily activities. When the called person would respond to the family member that beckoned them, they would be surprised to find out that the family member was completely oblivious to the event. It wasn't until Marie was home alone and heard her name called out by what sounded like one of her daughters that she realized this was abnormal. It was especially weird since the children were at a relative's house! The fact that something else was in the home with her and her children terrified her.

This is a common thing reported in hauntings. In many cases, it is thought that the spirits use familiar sounds in hopes of attracting attention. In most situations, the spirit just wants to be noticed and acknowledged—and what better way to get a reaction than saying a name?

One of the most unusual reports came from her boyfriend, Mike. He had claimed seeing footprints leading up to the home. Alarmed, he asked Marie if the kids play outside on that side of the house; she said no. Mike thought it was weird that the tracks leading up to the windows didn't have tracks going in the opposite direction. It was almost as if whatever came up to the home never left. Mike was scared; as a police officer, he knew much about society's troubled individuals.

Seeing the footprints was not Mike's only encounter with the activity, but as a skeptic, he tried to rationalize the events so he could grasp what was happening.

One morning while getting into his truck to leave for the office, Mike glanced in the rearview mirror as he yawned. He saw a black figure walk behind his truck from left to right. His head quickly shot to the driver's side window, expecting to see Marie walk up to his window, but there was nothing there but the grayness of the foggy morning. He got out of his truck to make sure it was not one of the kids but found nothing. A bit shaken, he quickly pulled out of the driveway and hoped that his morning at work would make him forget what he had seen.

As our investigation started that night, Marie was so shaken up that she tossed us the keys to this beautiful home and told us to lock up when we were done. She wanted no part in the activity—she had lived through enough!

Our investigation was quite normal; we only captured EVPs in our findings. Our equipment was quite less advanced than it is today—we had only EMF meters, audio recorders, and cameras for photos.

Late in the night, we locked up the house and headed home. I was still shocked and surprised over the talk with Marie in the living room. It was the highlight of the investigation because it yielded results I truly did not expect.

A few days after our night at the Saddle home, I received a call from Monica, who was in a surprised mood herself. She had just hung up the phone with Marie and had some exciting news.

"Are you sitting down?" she asked me.

"Yeah. Why?" I asked.

"I just got off the phone with Marie and she had some interesting news to share with us. She was talking with her cousin who used to live at the home. She asked if there ever was a Ralph or Charlie who lived there, and her cousin admitted that she used to have an imaginary friend named Ralph. She claimed he was a farmer," Monica had said. "I thought you would like to know that."

I said thanks with a somber tone as I hung up the phone. The investigation night had been enough to floor me, but the fact that I was now batting 100 percent on my first night out as a psychic was too much for me to comprehend.

I do not perform any more psychical experiments as I did in this case. While my experience was positive, this approach does not provide data free from human contamination. Today, all of our evidence is from an objective perspective; if we capture video, anyone can review and attempt to recreate it. You can't do that with a psychic approach!

About a week after the investigation, we made plans to revisit the Saddle home and present Marie with our findings. I asked her how things were going, and she said they have been interesting. I gave her a CD copy of our audio findings and asked her to give me a call if she had any questions. She said she did not want to listen to them by herself but appreciated the gesture. She wanted to know our honest feelings on the home. While we never did get conclusive evidence other than the strange audio, the night was quite interesting. The home had its oddities, and I had no answer for my experiment's success.

I explained to Marie that this was her home and a place where her and her family should feel safe. These entities, including the pervasive shadow figure, posed no real threat to them. The spirits were simply occupying the same space, and she should make it clear that they were not to interfere with her family's space. Stating aloud the rules of the home to the areas of activity and stresssing that not following these "house rules" would result in banishment has proven very successful in our cases.

We never did get a second chance to investigate this home; the family eventually moved. Mike and Marie became closer, and the family relocated to his house. I still keep in touch with Marie, and she has asked me a few times if she can tag along with our group on an investigation, which is great to hear. She has overcome her fears and has moved on with her life.

I often still wonder about this home and whether the new residents experience unseen occupants, and if the little girl in the closet has finally found someone who wants to play with her and not ask so many stupid questions.

13

IT GROWLED AT ME

Just after Halloween 2005, Monica brought me a case involving her friends. She explained to me that this case was to be kept off the record, which is something we sometimes do in extreme cases when the family is worried about privacy or something really unusual. This case was my first case that dealt with "something" that went far beyond ghosts, and due to this, the case never happened according to our public records. This is my first public recollection of that night, and yes, I have changed the names and geographic information.

Nestled in a small residential neighborhood, the Tanner family (no, not the famous TV family that had a full house) had problems hidden from neighbors. Proud business owners Sandy and Greg were two grandparents who saw their oldest son, Allen, take a trip down drug alley and into rehab. While he was there, they took in his teenage son, Michael, and applied for his custody, which they were able to get. Once Allen was out of rehab, they took him into their home, but he soon relapsed.

Allen was a rough-and-tumble type character who got into trouble and thought he would be young forever. He had no responsibilities, and in his mind, his stay with his family was just always temporary. His parents knew better and wanted the best for him while having to watch him self-destruct.

Michael was a typical teenage geek. He was tall and skinny and had red hair and acne. His troubles with his dad stigmatized him and attracted the wrong type of crowd. His grandparents tried to keep him from the same mistakes that his father made. Michael was caught in two different upbringings: Michael's grandparents were calm and respectful while his dad was the wild child who didn't care much for authorifty. Michael never knew which way to go, and because of this, the doctors pronounced him as bipolar and were quick to dispense medication.

The mocha-colored home they lived in was a typical "square home" with rooms in each of the four corners one had to walk through in a circle to navigate. The living room, dining room, kitchen, and entry were all on the main floor, while the three bedrooms and bath were on the second. The home had a small basement with a washroom and storage within its white stone walls.

One night while sleeping, Sandy was awakened to the feeling of fingers around her neck choking her. She struggled to wake her husband up and once he finally did, the fingers vanished. As Sandy tried to catch her breath, her husband searched the home from top to bottom only to find Michael asleep and Allen absent. The deadbolt on the door was still in the locked position.

As someone who didn't believe in ghosts, Greg comforted his wife before going back to sleep. They forgot about the incident until Michael spoke about the oddities in his room one morning at breakfast.

"Last night, Steve and I were making a fort out of blankets in my room. We had the blanket on my dresser and bed," Michael explained. "Then all of a sudden, the dresser lifted up and levitated above us!"

"Oh that's nonsense!" Greg exclaimed unwilling to share his wife's harrowing experience with their grandson. "I bet you guys were just tired."

"No, it really happened! Ask Ste—" Michael tried to say but was interrupted by his grandmother.

"Well, next time, just let us know when it happens," Sandy said while eyeing Greg nervously. "We'll look into it."

A few days later, Michael called the couple upstairs.

"Do you hear that?" he nervously asked his grandparents.

"Hear what?" Greg replied.

"That growling!" Michael said in a panic. "I was on my way to the bathroom and I heard this growling coming from your bedroom. Can't you hear it?"

"Yes, I can…" Sandy said with hesitation. "What is that?" She pushed the door open to their bedroom and the noises stopped.

At this point, the family was starting to become scared. They knew something was wrong in the home but were unsure of what it was. They decided to keep everything between them—until Michael's life was put in danger.

Michael was up in his room one night, sitting against the door with a friend, a girl. The two teens were discussing the signatures Michael had on his door, left by various friends who decided to literally leave their mark.

"Do you like Alicia?" the girl asked him.

"She's okay but I never really talk to her. Why?" Michael replied.

"Well, I heard she is thinking of asking Dylan out to the junior dan—" the girl said before she was interrupted by a knife sticking into the door between them.

"Did you throw that?!" Michael yelped at her.

"How could I? I was over here with you!" she replied.

Both of them decided to leave the room and go talk to Sandy, who was downstairs in the kitchen. Once they explained what had happened, the girl decided that she'd had enough and left. Michael did not return to his room until Greg got home from work, he was so frightened.

After that, the family decided that they needed to contact my team. Sandy was fed up and wanted to find out how we could help her and her family out. She was scared, and did not know where to turn.

We arrived at the home in early November, and we had yet to see snow. It was cold, and the wind was picking up as the grayness of winter dulled the early afternoon. The team was greeted by the family and given a tour of the home, which is usually how we start investigations.

Once we had begun, I decided to go upstairs to investigate with Garrett, a member of the team. This was one of his first client investigations and he was a bit nervous. When we got to the bedroom, I did a quick scan for baseline readings with the EMF. I noticed that in the hallway, as I approached Sandy and Greg's bedroom, the meter showed an increase in EMF reading.

We poked open the door and measured the room but were surprised at what greeted us in there.

I scanned the bed and on the left side, I noticed a higher reading than the right side. As I scanned around, I grabbed Garrett by the shoulder.

"Quiet…Do you hear that?" I asked him.

"Yeah, I hear something. It sounds like an animal wheezing," he replied in a whisper. I thought this was interesting, given the reports of growling coming from the bedroom.

I leaned down to measure the EMF under the bed when I noticed the animal noise getting louder. I knew that in my research about negative entities some are not keen on people who are not afraid of them. They thrive on the energy and emotion fear causes, and when they realize you aren't going to allow them to have that, they get nervous. You end up turning the tables on them.

"You know that we aren't afraid of you," I said out loud and with confidence. "The family is pissed off that you are here, and that's why we are here."

The growling grew louder.

"You sound like an angry rat," I said in disgust. "We will not tolerate your actions to the family anymore."

I bent over to check under the bed where the growling was coming from to make sure it was not just a cat or something the family had forgotten to tell us. When I lifted the bedspread, a whoosh of air rushed past me with great force and into the closet. It left the clothing on hangers jostling.

I looked over at Garrett, and his eyes were huge. He definitely saw whatever caused it! I grabbed the EMF meter and headed for the closet. The readings were high, but the growling had stopped.

The rest of the room was pretty low in EMF at this point so we went downstairs to tell the others on the team what we experienced. Naturally, they wanted to check it out themselves so another team including Monica and Nancy went upstairs.

It wasn't long until my name was called to come upstairs. When I reached the two ladies, they were in Michael's room with the dowsing rods, two L-shaped metal pieces. When we use dowsing rods, we treat them as a way for spirits to communicate with us or as low-budget EMF meters. They usually swing in a slow fashion from right or left but in this case, they were spinning fast and in complete circles like helicopter blades.

I called the family upstairs to allow them to witness this so they could see that their experiences were not so far-fetched. There was something abnormal in this house, and with the experience Garrett and I had earlier, I asked the family a simple question:

"Have you ever used a Ouija board in the home?"

"No, never…I don't even allow them," Sandy exclaimed. Looking at Michael, I knew the story was different.

"Well…I did once…with my friends," he shyly confessed.

Sandy was in shock and disbelief. She had tried so hard to keep her home under her rules.

"Where at?" I asked.

"The dining room on the table," he said pointing down.

The dining room was right below Michael's bedroom and would have explained the vortex of energy causing the rods to spin in a vigorous fashion.

Often times when an Ouija board is used within a home, the affected areas are vertically related to the space where the board's communication was conducted. Imagine a spotlight being pointed up in the air and how the light penetrates the darkness. The energy from the board does the same, and if not closed properly, creates a place for wandering spirits to gather and congregate. I once heard a theory about how spirits can be very transient and move around our world like vagrants. Imagine an apocalyptic movie (zombies for example) where the survivors move around looking for others they can gather with. As humans, we are social creatures; the old adage of "you are in death as you were in life" proves true, which means ghosts congregate. When you have a vortex of energy, it can gather entities like bugs to a streetlight. If something darker came through, it would remain close to this energy source. Sure enough, the grandparents' bedroom was just across the hall.

The family was in complete disbelief at how their lives were affected and how something marketed as a game could wreak so much havoc.

We advised the family to consult with a local clergy member with whom they felt comfortable. Our stance has always been that we do not eliminate spirits, nor are we demonologists. We handle ghosts that were human at one point. While our journeys do sometimes cross paths with other entities (shadow people, darker energies, elementals, etc.), we try to draw the line at entities that were at one time human. While it may seem contradictory, I have taken very basic steps to inform my team on how to differentiate cases that involve these darker entities for each member's safety and in instances when we need to draw the line.

When dealing with cases featuring darker energies, we usually ask that the client consult with a clergy member with whom they feel familiar because we are not properly trained to perform certain religious rites. These clergy members will often meet with the family to provide religious consulting, prayers, and possibly a blessing ritual at the home.

In my years consulting on ghost cases, I have stumbled upon many people in the field who claim to be ghost hunters and demonologists. I cannot stress enough how bad a decision and how dangerous it can prove to be. Demonology is a much more serious course of study and one that should not be taken lightly as demons are much more harmful than ghosts. After all, they thrive on torture and fear.

In cases that deal with darker energies, I don't like to lay out all my cards publicly because it helps me distinguish true cases from the less than honest ones. The best way I can generically state the differences between a case involving a ghost and a case involving a darker energy is that a darker case has negative results on the living's behavior within the home. A ghost will just annoy you and try to get your attention.

I still find myself thinking about the Tanner family from time to time, even though I have lost contact with them. I wonder how they are doing and reflect that it's hard to believe just how much the paranormal can affect peoples' normal lives.

14

A SPIRITED BED AND BREAKFAST

The thing the television programs wish they could capture but almost always fail to show is the true relationship between a client and an investigator. In the early winter of 2006, I found out how much of an effect what I do has on the people I help. I would learn this lesson when our team returned to the quaint town of New Ulm to investigate a small bed and breakfast.

I was contacted by the owner, Shelly, who told me that her family lived in the bed and breakfast and that her two young girls were experiencing something terrifying in their rooms which prevented them from sleeping at night. She asked if we were willing to help out. Just like my counter-parts at The Atlantic Paranormal Society (TAPS), when kids are involved, I make it a priority to help out if I am able.

The family lived on the third floor of the historic inn and operated the lower two floors as the bed and break-fast. The entire building featured ornamental woodwork-ing, historical photos, and really did a great job of taking guests back to years long gone. Where most people would expect a hotel with a swimming pool, this bed and break-fast brought you to a time when families would entertain passing guests by being social and hospitable.

The daughters' experience was frightening enough to ask us for our assistance. The daughters shared a room that was an offshoot of their parents' bedroom. The youngest daughter, Kayla, claimed that every night, a man stood in her doorway and said his name was Jacob. She said "Jacob" would never cross into their room but rather lean up against the door frame and watch the girls. He had a wound on his chest he would try to cover up from the girls so as not to alarm them.

Kayla also said there was another man in the room with her. Shelly explained to us that Kayla told her his name was Ralph. She explained that he had very old boots on that she compared to a pirate's buccaneer boots. He was a mean-spir-ited man, and she thought Jacob was there because of this strange man; they seemed to know each other.

Shelly told me that she didn't want to have the kids around when my team arrived and didn't want them to know about our investigation within the home. It was nothing against us but rather the fact that she wanted to know if Kayla was experiencing something real or imaginary.

Shelly agreed with her husband that he would take the young girls hunting with him; the deer hunting season in Minnesota had recently began. This gave our team a chance to investigate the property for a weekend.

I was excited to be back in New Ulm. The town offered my team previous cases that were historically fascinating and fun to uncover. The town itself has interesting roots, and the history that created New Ulm is very interesting. In 1862, the Dakota Sioux were upset at the United States government, and decided to burn the town to the ground—twice.

I was also excited to get involved with this case in New Ulm because it gave me an opportunity to work with my good friend, Mary Kay. She was a psychic who had worked with us on a previous case in New Ulm and one of the few psychics I trusted. Lucky for us, she lived in the town.

Shelly had mentioned that her youngest daughter was seeing ghosts, which meant there might be a chance that Kayla had some psychic talents. Our investigation would give Mary Kay and Shelly an opportunity to meet. Because Mary Kay lived locally, the family now had a reliable resource if there were problems in the future.

The team for this case would consist of Monica, Kelly, Nancy, and myself.

When we entered the home, Shelly was very hospitable; running a bed and breakfast was a good choice for her. She was the perfect host and explained the events in a very cheerful manner to my team during our tour. You would not have known that this woman was scared out of her mind in her own home. I had previously asked Mary Kay to show up an hour after the team so we could keep her out of the history of the home as much as possible.

After the team wrapped up the tour, Shelly explained to us that she had the abstract of the property available, which was a pleasant surprise. For those who don't know, an abstract of a property lists the names of the owners, dates they owned the property, and usually for how much the property sold. We agreed that we would start our investigation and refer to the abstract if we needed to later, as we did not want the historical information to lead Mary Kay's psychic suggestions. In other words, we wanted to be as cold to the historical information as the psychic so no one would tip her off.

We broke into two teams. My team headed to the basement to conduct baseline readings. While down there, I noticed that the floor was dirt in spots and that there was a high EMF field near the top of the ceiling. Old wiring had been neglected in the past, a health risk for anyone in the basement. (If we don't find ghosts, we at least can give clients an idea of whether their wiring is good or bad based on EMF readings!)

While in the basement, I turned to Monica, who was with me, and said, "It feels like you could get away with anything down here." I am not sure why I said that, but the dark confines of the cluttered basement seemed like the spot where secrets would be kept. She shrugged it off, and we continued our investigation in the basement.

Once we had gathered with the rest of the team, we shared our ideas and thoughts on the location. Much of the team agreed that they wanted to come back here just to spend the weekend—the rooms were gorgeous and well decorated.

Shelly caught up with us and asked what we had found so far. While we were doing our baseline readings, she was seeing off the guests who were spending the night at the inn, giving them tips on various nightlife and restaurants. The inn was empty. Only my team and the owner were left to find any signs of life within the building.

"So, what did you think of the place?" Shelly asked. It must always be nerve-wracking to see how your business stacks up to the expectations of visitors who are used to elevators and electronic key cards.

"It's a great place, and you have done a wonderful job here," I replied.

"Find anything yet?" she inquired.

Even though we were only about an hour into it, Monica made mention of what I said to her in the basement.

"That's really odd that you mention that, because when I used to smoke, I didn't want my husband to find out, so I would go into the basement to smoke. When we were cleaning down there a few years ago, we also found a lot of old whiskey bottles."

"I also found it weird how there is a dirt floor in one section when the majority of it is concrete," Shelly confessed. "We had one psychic here who explained to us that there was an energy vortex over that spot, whatever that means."

At this point and with perfect timing, Mary Kay walked through the door and we introduced her to Shelly. We took her on a brief tour of the home to get her impressions and so she could understand the building's layout.

We were in the basement when Mary Kay walked to the dirt section of the floor and made mention that there was something unusual about this spot—it seemed to hum with energy. I had previously decided to reserve what Shelly told us about the energy vortex until after our investigation.

"Have you ever dug in this spot?" Mary Kay asked Shelly.

"No, never thought of doing that," Shelly stated. "Why?"

"There is something here related to the spirits that are here," Mary Kay said. "Maybe bones?"

"Oh man, I never thought of that before," Shelly said with a nervous tone. Looking at me, she asked, "Do you really think that is maybe what is there?"

I shrugged, "Could be a possibility, but who knows?"

As we began to investigate the rest of the building, we found ourselves on the third floor in the children's bedroom. Mary Kay hesitated and stopped before entering the room.

"There is someone who likes to stand here," she said while moving her hands in a circle as if she was washing an invisible piece of glass. "It's a man."

We all watched her as she started to pick up on the trail of the reported activity. It was quite amazing to watch her work.

"There is another man who sits across the room. These two know each other and are responsible for each other being here," Mary Kay whispered with her eyes closed. She was starting to focus more on the relationship between these two men. "The gentleman that stands here was stabbed in the chest."

"The other man's name starts with an R…like 'Ray,' but it's not Ray," said Mary Kay. "He's the reason why this other man was stabbed. A fight occurred and this man who stands here is afraid of this guy with the R name. That's why he never enters."

Shelly was in disbelief, as was the rest of my team. Mary Kay had no knowledge of the family or the situation that had led us here, but she had explained everything to a T. I decided it was time to take a break, gather the team, and change our mode from spectator to investigation.

While having coffee and hot cocoa in the kitchen area, Shelly asked me if I would like to see the abstract from the property. I agreed that it might be a good idea to see if the property had mentioned Jacob and a gentleman with an R name. The question was not "Are these things being picked up in the environment?" but rather "Were these real people?"

Looking at the abstract, I found that there was a listing of property being sold from an R. Watson to a Jacob Smith in the late 1880s. The property remained with Jacob Smith for about a year, after which it was transferred back to R. Watson.

Why was it transferred back to the original owner after a year? Was R. Watson the strange man who appeared next to Kayla's bed? Was this the man who might have killed Jacob Smith after a foul dealing?

We can only hypothesize about the situation in history, but it was one of the more shocking moments in my career to have similar facts show up in the property's background. It is at this moment that you not only read history but realize that it is very real and reaching.

After finding this, I started to think more about the dirt flooring in the basement. I recalled Shelly mentioning that this home had a psychic in it before who said they were dealing with an energy vortex. As stated in earlier chapters, vortex activity usually affects the property vertically.

"Shelly, can I ask you something? I inquired. "What's above that spot with the dirt flooring in the basement?"

"That's the kitchen area," she replied. "Why?"

"Well, what's above that?" I pressed further.

"A hallway."

"And above that?"

"My daughters' bedroom…" Shelly said with a slight pause. "More specifically, the door to my daughters' bedroom…Oh, you don't think that has something to do with this, do you?"

"It could be a possibility," I put forth. "Anything is possible in a situation like this."

In my experiences with what many call vortices, I have found that they act like vertical beams of light and affect anything in a vertical relation to the source. It keeps the activity within a ten- to fifteen-foot radius of this beam.

We decided Mary Kay would try to communicate with Jacob and ask him to leave because he was scaring the girls. I decided to run an audio recorder while she did this so we might be able to hear him talking to her, if possible.

Mary Kay spoke to Jacob as though he was right in the room with her, expressing both compassion and frustration. It was quite a sight for our team to see. She mentioned that Jacob had stuck around to watch the girls so that the man with the R name wouldn't hurt them, and the two spirits were like yin and yang to each other. Once she convinced Jacob that it was time to go, she mentioned that a dog came out of "the light" to greet him and he eventually left.

There was not much the non-psychics witnessed other than Mary Kay's commentary on the situation which would have been hard for the skeptic to believe. I had a hard time telling the client that Jacob was really gone because I couldn't confirm it.

As the night wrapped up, we were tired and had about an hour's ride back to our comfy beds. We gathered our gear and left the home the way that we found it. As we started to walk out to our vehicles to load them up, Shelly followed us out and talked with us.

We said our goodbyes, and as with all clients, I let her know I would be in touch. I extended my hand for a handshake, and Shelly lunged forward and gave me a tight hug.

"Thank you very much. I am glad there are people out there like you," she whispered in my ear. I could tell tears were starting to well up in her eyes.

I didn't know what to say because I had never had a client do this before so I patted her on the back. As she let go of me, she wiped the tears off her face and smiled to hide her emotions. The rest of the team gave her a soft smile because they understood how hard this was for her.

It wasn't until a few days later while analyzing the audio from the recorder when I noticed something odd. While I was unable to hear the conversation from Jacob's end, I heard something strange: when he supposedly passed into the light, there was the sound of a grandfather clock chiming as if it were midnight. We asked for a sign of his passing, and the odd thing is that we did this at 1:20 in the morning. The other odd thing is that there aren't any clocks in the building that would have made that sound.

I can't explain it.

Even now, I still do my best to keep in touch with Shelly and check in on her family to see how the girls are doing. There have been no reports of Jacob in the home since our night there, but the family did invite my good friends at the Minnesota Paranormal Investigators Group to check out other spirits the family believes reside within the home.

The truly amazing and beautiful moments of ghost hunting come from clients like Shelly. These are the people who don't know which way to turn and find some comfort in the fact that sincere and dedicated people are out there to help them. All those nights in the dark looking for answers and the sleeplessness are well worth it for moments like the one Shelly shared with me.

15

THE GREYHOUND BUS MUSEUM

Sometimes the best cases come from very strange places. In 2008, my team would be lucky enough to have what would become one of our favorite cases from a sea of random people.

During the Field of Screams haunted maze event in Chisholm, a man approached our team's booth. He was dressed in black from head to toe. He had on a black baseball hat that, along with his dark beard, appeared to sandwich his glasses. He was wearing a black leather jacket, cowboy boots, and black jeans. We could tell this guy was pretty hardcore—after all, he looked like Mad Max.

"So uh, you guys look for ghosts, huh?" the stranger said to us.

"Yeah! Why, you got one?" replied Don, a member of MNPSG at the time.

"You could say that. I work at the Greyhound Museum in Hibbing," the man said. "Do you know where that is? It's in North Hibbing."

Don reached over and tried pulling at me to come over from the group of kids listening to an EVP file on one of our laptops. I tried brushing him off, but he persisted, knowing I was the person to talk to about haunted museums.

Don introduced the two of us with a nervously excited tone, adding the stranger's claim of having ghosts in their museum.

I asked the sharply dressed stranger what was going on there. I am always very hard to impress when it comes to ghost stories, as I have heard some real great "stories" from people who simply want attention.

"Well, I work at Greyhound and do maintenance and stuff there. I'm the assistant director."

My eyes lit up. I knew this guy was not just another random storyteller; he was head of staff at the museum and could actually get us into the location. One thing you have to realize about these events is that when we get case leads, a lot of them are just people telling us about this far-out rural location they don't have access or permission to get us into. It's a lot of "well, there's this old abandoned building, and if you went into it, you'd probably get yourself killed, but it is totally haunted!" By contrast, the gentleman before us now was serious about his story. He had connections and the means to get us to the location.

"Every morning when I get in there, I find things out of place. My tools are rearranged in my locked toolbox, my manuals are taken out of my locked box and stacked on top of it, bus windows open on their own, doors close by themselves…my workers are scared and don't want to be in there!" the man said, trying to keep his voice above the loud crowd behind him. "My name is Glen."

I told him that we would love to check it out and wrote down his info. We decided to take him up on his offer a few months later, in January.

As with all cases, we send out one or two members of the team to interview and tour the location. We do this to assess whether the place is safe for our team and equipment, and we like to make sure the story checks out. We also conduct repeat interviews with different people to make sure the story doesn't change.

I decided to tour the Greyhound Bus Origin Museum because…well, because I love museums! I am a history fanatic and love seeing artifacts. I'm especially fascinated by the odd history of a location relevant to me such as in Hibbing.

Here is what I had learned about the museum and its history:

The Greyhound Bus Origin Museum is dedicated to the Swedish immigrants who started a taxi company in Hibbing that eventually became America's largest transportation company. The company was started in 1914 when Carl Wickman was laid off as a miner. He noticed that his fellow miners had a tough time getting to and from work, so he decided to go into business to taxi them around. His first vehicle was a Hupmobile. Eventually, he took on a partner in Andrew "Bus Andy" Anderson and the two formed Mesaba Transportation in 1915. Eventually the two sold their business. In 1933, it became the Greyhound Bus Corporation and went national.

In the late 1960s, the museum came to be when a citizen of Hibbing named Gene Nicolelli found a plaque that stated that Greyhound Bus was started in Hibbing. He gave the plaque to the Hibbing Public Library but they lost it. It turned up again in 1973, and Gene was not going to let it go missing again. He took it as his duty to preserve the history of Greyhound's birth in Hibbing.

Well, eventually Gene found a home for his museum in the Hibbing Memorial Building's smallest corner. As one can imagine, it did not take long for the buses to outgrow that space; he needed more room. Funding was hard to come by, but eventually a governor granted him enough money for a new building wherever Gene wanted in Hibbing.

He picked an area on First Avenue, one of Mesaba Transportation's first routes. This spot was also next to a cemetery—the oldest cemetery in Hibbing.

In 1999, the museum had a new home, and the city even named the street it was on "Greyhound Boulevard." There is not one entrance into Hibbing that doesn't have a Greyhound Museum sign with their dog logo pointing the way to the building.

When I arrived at the museum for the first time in January of 2009, I went to the back shop and noticed a "Dawg Pound" sign above the door. After seeing the assistant director, Glen, dressed up as Mad Max and now this new discovery, I knew that the people who worked here were pretty intense.

I knocked on the large steel door.

No answer.

I knocked again, a bit harder, and waited for someone to yell at me for pounding on their door.

Then the door opened up and a man covered in paint with a long beard answered. He had his light hair in a ponytail and a very distinguished face. This was not the man from the Field of Screams we had met. Quite frankly, his hardened exterior scared me a bit. The inside of the shop was covered with plastic sheets, and two buses created long corridors. The smell of enamel paint filled my noise.

"Is Glen here?" I asked with a slight lump in my throat. This was more intense than actual investigating and to be fair, I was also trying to recover from the overpowering paint fumes.

"Hey Adam! I'm up here!" a familiar voice said to me as the ponytailed man walked away. I spotted Glen. He was on the roof of a bus that was undergoing some painting. Once I entered the shop, he climbed off the bus, wiped his hands on a rag, and shook my hand.

"Glad ya could make it! We got such a mess now since the museum's closed. We're in restoration mode for all the buses," Glen said. "C'mon, let me show you around."

We left the shop area and went into the museum's west entrance. As we entered the building, I noticed that we were now in a large room with several buses. There must have been six buses from Greyhound's past in that space.

"Here are our buses. These are the ones I was telling you about," Glen explained. "Every morning when I get here, I come in this room. The doors are supposed to be open, and the windows are supposed to be shut."

We walked around the room and took a look at the buses with a few stops to fix out-of-place windows and doors. I was impressed with the history of the buses and the mannequins lined up to board one bus. This wasn't my first time dealing with creepy mannequins on a location and probably won't be the last.

After we fixed the windows and doors in the bus room for display, Glen and I walked into the museum's main lobby. This area has a tile floor and a small double-sided bench in the center. There is a mannequin standing up at a mock ticket counter with a bell and clock. The walls are adorned with plaques of the donors for the museum and various awards the museum has received. Along one wall is a gift shop with a glass case featuring various souvenirs.

"This is another room that has a lot of activity. See all those name tags on that plaque? Notice how they are all different colors like bronze, silver, and gold? When I come in here, sometimes they are all switched around," Glen said. "They shouldn't be."

We then walked into the office where an older gentleman was sitting. He was wearing a light yellow button-down shirt and brown pants. From my research, I recognized him as Gene Nicolelli, the man responsible for putting together this museum.

"Adam, this is Gino Nicolelli. He is the director of the museum," said Glen. "Gino, this is the guy I told you about. The ghost hunter. You know that TV show on Syfy? Like that."

"Ah yes, sit down. Let's talk," Gene replied in a quiet voice as he shook my hand.

As we conversed, I could tell that Gene was serious in his inquiries about bringing my team into the museum. He stared at me pensively while sitting in his chair. He had his hands together so that only the fingertips touched.

I explained what we do, and told him that my team doesn't try to do anything other than document reported activity. I asked him about his experiences at the museum and he admitted that he was quite a skeptical person, which was great.

"I've never had anything happen to me," Gene said. "Glen and some other staff have reported some things happening like doors closing on their own and windows opening. I think Glen has mentioned that there was something about a toolbox, too?"

"Yeah," Glen interjected. "I was working on putting a new transmission in one of the buses. I couldn't figure out how to take it apart. I was frustrated, so I put all my books back into my toolbox. When I came back the next day, on my main drawer that I use for a shelf was the manual, open to the page I needed.

"I thought, Marshall, the other mechanic, was in after me. I called him up and said thanks because I was really baffled on this tranny. He asked me what I was talking about and he said, 'Glen, I'm in the hospital.' He had gone in that night due to a blood clot in his leg. I thought ... 'well, that's a little creepy!'"

After our talk in Gene's office, we decided to go take a look at the other portions of the museum. We walked back into the bus room where we had previously been. Things were a bit off.

I noticed that some doors were shut and a few windows had dropped down. I was trying to remain skeptical of this place; these were old buses, after all. We continued walking down the front of the buses to check out the "damage done." There was such a random hodgepodge of open and shut doors and windows that it seemed like something was trying to get my attention.

"See, this is what makes me mad," Glen said with frustration. "It's little stuff like this. We just got done fixing this!"

My hearty skeptical outlook died when I noticed that a cargo hatch door on the newest bus had been opened. Glen approached it and showed me how this was supposed to be a locked section of the bus.

"I'm the only one with keys to this," Glen said with a nervous tone in his voice. "And you see, you have to lock it to shut it."

He relocked the cargo hatch. Right then and there, I agreed to have our team investigate the location.

A few days later, we arrived as a team at the museum with our equipment cases. Glen opened the museum, and we unpacked our gear in the lobby, using the bench as a table. I knew that this was a large area we needed to cover with cameras. With the reported movement of the bus doors and windows, we needed to try to cover as much ground as possible.

I introduced everyone to Glen as we started to unpack. I had mentioned to Glen that we were going to use this place as a testing ground for a new approach for MinnesotaGhosts.com; this was the first place we would shoot our investigation webisodes. The webisodes are our way to show our visitors how the team conducts investigations and allows viewers to experience the activity with us. Basically, it was our attempt at putting together a small TV show-like episode on our website. Glen had agreed to this so our first thing to focus on was to shoot the interview and tour.

With Glen as our guide, the team walked through the museum as he talked about various items and historical treasures. (I won't go into every detail as this video is still available through our website.)

Glen ushered us into the large bus room that we had been in on my tour with him earlier that week. He mentioned the history of the buses to everyone and gave them the rundown on how things are supposed to be for display purposes; doors open, windows shut. We found a few windows that had been opened already.

"See, this is what I mean again," Glen said in an angry tone. "It is this stuff that gets me frustrated."

We started to help Glen shut the windows and found these windows hard to operate due to the rubber seals being removed. What's odd about these is that they usually make a lot of noise with the plastic clips being pushed in and out, but no one has ever reported hearing them open up.

We continued to film our tour with Glen, and eventually we had two cameras on him talking about his paranormal experiences at the location. He mentioned a story that was a bit offsetting, about a little girl seen roaming the grounds during the early morning hours. She is believed to be from the cemetery south of the museum.

"We have a lot of volunteers here, and they always mention how spooky that cemetery is and how they see a little girl in there. In the northwest corner, you will see a little kid in there," Glen said with a soft tone. "I always thought my daughter was crazy. She used to work at the nearby nursing home and they would tell stories about the patients there. Little old ladies would come out and steal the nurses' candy and when asked what they did with it, they'd say that they gave it to a little girl. I used to hear these stories and think it was all made up until one night…I saw that little girl.

"I know it isn't just me who saw her; I've heard Gino say he saw her too. I even know a Hibbing police officer has seen her. And the kid is not from this era—she's in an old-fashioned dress. It kinda freaked me out. I had to back up my truck after driving into work that morning, around 5 a.m. When I backed up, she wasn't standing there anymore."

Now the entire team was engaged and interested in his story.

"What was she dressed like?" asked Don.

"Blackish hair…pinkish kinda dress…and this was at like 4:30 in the morning so you know there aren't any kids out at that time. I even had a friend on the Hibbing PD who called me up one morning because she saw the little girl. I guess a lot of people have seen her but nobody wants to talk about it," Glen remarked uncomfortably.

"How old do you think she might be, about?" Don inquired.

"Oh I don't know…nine, ten?" Glen answered with a slight pause. You could tell he was vividly reminded of that scary experience once more.

I could tell by the quietness of the large room that the entire team was all set on capturing evidence of this little girl. You could hear the hum of the halogen lamps above us, it was so quiet. Glen went on to explain a bit about the history of the property and its relation to the little girl.

"This summer, we did a lot of history research on that cemetery. What's weird is that the northwest corner along our property line is nothing but little kids who died in the 1918 pandemic of yellow fever. I think the oldest one is nine years old."

One investigator who was out with us for the first time was floored by this story and the realism of ghosts sank in. It affects kids just as much as adults.

Glen then spoke about the history of the property the museum sits on.

"The location of this museum used to be an old play field. It was a baseball field. When the pandemic came through in 1918, they turned it into a pandemic camp for the sick. When people would die, they would put them into mass graves in the cemetery. You know all those squares without markers that are all just grass? Those are mass graves."

Glen told us about the buses in the main museum building. There were six buses used for various endeavors such as transporting troops from both world wars, a more modern bus, and a bus that was originally from 1927. The pure amount of history these buses held is fascinating in itself. Perhaps we were dealing with someone who used to be a passenger on one of the buses.

We asked Glen what he thought about the ghosts that inhabit the museum. He said, "I think there are old drivers here or mechanics. How else would it have known to open that book to the page I needed?"

Well, whoever or whatever was there, *we* were there to try to catch it pulling pranks.

We started to set up our equipment; we pulled out tripods, loaded tapes into cameras, set up a DVR unit we were borrowing from a friend, and made sure we had fresh batteries in all of our equipment.

Since we were also shooting video that would detail our adventure that night, we made sure to check how far we could get away from the camera in the dark before it all went black. In all honesty, this was something that we didn't know much about; we were flying by the seat of our pants.

We went "lights out" which means ... well, we turned off all the lights in the building except for command central, in the lobby. This place left its security lights on.

Don and Mick started out as a team, as did Kristin and I. Don and Mick sat in the trophy room with the glass cases to see if they could get some EVP audio done. Kristin and I headed into the room with the buses, and sat on the bus called the Scenicruiser.

The Scenicruiser had two levels to it and featured large, brown leather seats. It also had a narrow aisle I kept bumping into with my hips, which made it hard to maneuver quietly.

I turned on my recorder and asked several questions such as "What is your name? How old are you? What year is it? Who is President? Where do you live?" Kristin said she did not feel well in the bus, so I asked if she wanted to get out. She said yes, and we decided to exit the bus. Once outside of it, she felt better. The odd thing is that upon playback the next day, we caught something telling us to "get out" while we were talking about Kristin not feeling well. She is spooked to this day and will not return to the Greyhound Bus Museum to sit on the buses.

When we regrouped with the team in the lobby, Don and Mick said they didn't think they got much recorded on audio; they could hear Kristin and me on the bus. It turned out that the acoustics in this location were going to be troublesome for audio evidence. We then decided that only one team would be able to go in at a time.

Glen had asked me earlier if it was all right if he tagged along with one of us to investigate. He was curious about the events that happened to him during his time working at the museum. Seeing him as a catalyst for activity, we agreed it might be good.

I decided to take Glen with me and board the buses one by one, sitting in the quiet dark. Now I will say that I am a bit fearful of these buses since in the darkness, you have glass on each side of you. One of the most frightening things that one can experience is something appearing in front of your face. Obviously there is not a lot of space on a bus, and it is the best opportunity to have something jump up in the window from the bus's sides.

We sat there in the dark on the Battle of Britain bus. Glen had a Cell Sensor EMF meter in one hand and I had the camera for our webisode. I asked the question, "Is there anyone in here who wants to make their presence known?" We received one brief and small spike on the meter. I asked Glen if he had moved the probe at all, he said no. I asked for another sign of a presence and nothing happened at all. Being skeptical of the situation, I reviewed the tape and saw that he did not move enough to trigger the device when the meter flashed.

We moved onto the Buffalo bus and sat there the same as we did on the Battle of Britain. I asked the same questions but nothing happened. We sat there for about five minutes and decided to move on—it was quiet peaceful on the bus. Glen stepped off before me; I was the last one off the bus. As soon as we exited the bus, Glen shouted that he saw a shadow dart off behind one of the buses! Since he was in front of me, my camera did not pick up what he just saw.

We ran over to the back of the bus where Glen had seen the shadow. There was nothing there, but we did hear something—a small rattling sound like metal. Looking around, we found that a piece of metal on one of the buses was making the sound. It was the engine compartment door that would be taken off by the Greyhound staff when putting a new engine in a bus. It was almost as if someone had run past this and kicked it. Something solid had hit this metal panel!

Fearing we were being pranked by my fellow investigators, we naturally started to ask questions as we started to walk back toward the lobby to see where everyone was.

"Is there someone back here?" Glen asked.

"Can you make it light up?" I asked. "Give us a sign of your presence. We are not here to hurt you."

No response.

"Is there somebody else in here with us?" Glen asked nervously. The anticipation was mounting.

"We're not trying to hurt you," I tried to say calmly in the dark, although my tone said differently.

In a faint whisper, Glen and I heard somebody say what appeared to be "go." We debated over this for a moment and really tried to grasp what was happening. I originally thought the voice belonged to Don since he was in the lobby.

Glen was now clearly shaken, and he asked a question that fit his mindset. "Do you want me to stop working at the museum?" he asked. "Or do you want us to just go for the night?"

Right after he asked the second question, Glen heard what appeared to be a whisper from somewhere in the dark say, "Night." He told me what he heard and asked me, "Did you hear that? 'Night.'" I did not hear this voice, but upon reviewing our evidence, I realized we captured the disembodied voice with the equipment.

Completely disturbed and trying to find the truth, we both decided to see who was in the lobby and what they had been recently discussing. We approached the lobby and found Kristin in front of the monitors (where she had stayed since feeling nauseous on the bus). Don was eating a Pop Tart, his snack for the midnight adventure. To me, this meant his mouth had been occupied for some time, and he was not the owner of the voice we had heard. He gratefully showed us his half-eaten treat on camera as Mick stepped out of the men's restroom. I asked Don if he had been talking and he answered that he had just come inside from smoking a cigarette. No one had said a word.

We were unable to find an answer for the disembodied voices we heard but were lucky enough to capture them. These are up for public listening on our website. We were able to capture a few more sounds we could not explain on the recorders.

Sometimes we do what is called "ambient audio" where we leave an audio recorder in a location of known activity. It can be a tedious task when it comes to evidence review, but it often leads to interesting finds; sometimes we record voices talking about us when we are not around. At the bus museum, we left one recorder by the latch that opens the bus door and captured what appears to be the sound of the lever arm moving. This noise seems to rock back and forth until the latch unlocked and the door came free to be shut. This would explain why the doors can shut despite being locked in the open position.

After the investigation, we presented Glen and the rest of the Greyhound staff with a DVD of our findings. They forwarded this on to the head of Greyhound Bus company, who was fascinated with the results. We were asked to come back and try to find more results, which we happily did on April 4, 2009.

For evidence purposes, this investigation was not as profound as our first, but we were able to have much more personal experiences. These personal experiences are something I know my team is not going to forget in their lifetimes.

The night in April started off much like the first investigation; we had set up our equipment and were able to go "lights out." We had agreed to let another staff member and his son stay with us for the night so they could learn about what we do.

The staff member was a stout but large man who dressed in a flannel shirt and shorts. His personality was laid back but when things got serious with him, you knew it. His son was a taller kid dressed in a hooded sweatshirt, also wearing shorts. He was quiet for the most part, but you could tell by his eyes that he was interested in what we were doing at the museum that night.

We started off the night by making sure that all the bus windows were shut like they should be and that the doors were all open as they would be for display. The museum was set to open in about a month, so this would be our last crack at the ghosts before they got released from their Minnesota winter "cabin fever." We were able to explore new outer buildings this time around because the snow had mostly melted.

The team was also set to use a piece of equipment called an infrared strobe that had never tested out before. I had first heard about this theory from my good friend Paul Bradford, the tech manager of Ghost Hunters International. He was originally testing it out and asked if we would be interested in testing it along with his television crew.

This device allowed us to put out what was like a beacon. In theory, it is thought that spirits can see light spectrums we cannot (such as IR lighting) and hopefully this beacon would attract a curious wanderer. After all, wouldn't you check out something as odd as a blinking light in the dark? The strobe also allows cameras to slow down movement, since it takes away half the visible video frames. At the time, it was just being tested by a few investigative groups in the field. We were proud to be one of those teams.

Mick, Don, and the worker's son were the first to investigate the bus room. We had just gone lights out, and the trio boarded the Buffalo. Don made a comment that he saw what appeared to be a shadow behind one of the buses when he was boarding the Buffalo. This is also where Glen had seen the shadow in January, something we thought was interesting. Don was pretty shaken but excited at the same time. Mick had already been on the bus and was teaching the worker's son about EMF meters and EVP recording techniques. As Don boarded the bus with camera in hand, Mick noticed that something was out of the ordinary...

"Hey Don...Don!" Mick said with a bit of confusion in his voice.

"Yes sir," Don replied.

"Is this one of the windows that couldn't be closed?" Mick asked.

"Dude, we just did a walkthrough and there wasn't a window open!" Don exclaimed. "We walked around every bus!"

"But you just said that you saw that shadow too?" Mick stated.

"Well, here is what we're gonna do..." Don said but was interrupted midsentence by Mick's laughing.

"Well, no, we got some K2 hits...big!" Mick exclaimed.

The K2 meter, a device used to measure electrical energy in the environment, was spiking in the worker's son's hands. Frantic to cover the action, Don grabbed his camera and rushed over to try to document the activity.

The team then decided to try to take some EVP audio from outside the bus where Don had claimed to see the shadow. The team thought they heard something while recording, and so they walked back toward the rear of the buses. Upon playback of their tape, Mick heard something unusual, so he passed it along to me. I synced up the audio with the video from Don's camera and found that the "voice" that we had heard was actually Don stepping on the mechanic's dry floor. We were glad to debunk this, and it just goes to show that you should always have two ways to gather evidence whenever possible.

Meanwhile in an exterior storage building, another trio was trying to gather evidence. Glen, the staff member, and myself were inside a building where another Buffalo was stored. They refer to this building as the "Montana Building."

When you walk into the Montana Building, you are immediately facing the rear driver's side of a bus. We walked toward the front of the bus, and I noticed that the driver's ticket window was open. This small window is along the driver's side and where the drivers will take passenger's tickets before allowing them to board the bus. In our first exploration of this museum in January, we actually had caught the sound of one of these small windows flying open on the other Buffalo bus. We caught it on our mini-DV video camera stationed nearby.

Before we even opened the bus door of the Buffalo bus, I asked for a sign of a presence. Now, I learned a very important lesson here: never ever go any place without a camera. I had left my video camera on its tripod to test out our IR strobe where Don and Mick were. The following experience could have been the best footage that I ever caught; both for hilarity and for paranormal experiences.

After asking for a sign of a presence, we heard small tapping sounds coming from inside the back of this bus. This sound happened whenever I would ask for a sign of its presence. I agreed that we would ask it some questions and it would knock twice for yes, and only once for no. As I was explaining the rules to the spirit, Glen had decided he was going to pop open the lock on this bus and climb aboard. This was a mistake—he was now encroaching on the spirit's turf without respect.

Glen had only reached as far as the top of the stairs before he got his warning to back off. He climbed aboard the bus, screaming and pissed off because this thing was messing with him. He jumped about two feet out of his work boots, scrambling for words.

"Oh…#$%@! I gotta get off this $%#@ing bus! I need a cigarette! That %$#@ing bathroom door just opened and slammed shut! I am a #$@%ing Marine! I am not supposed to be scared!" he yelled in a panic.

The only problem was that his staff member was standing in front of the bus, blocking our only way out. Glen tried to push him out of the way, but his coworker is built like a rock. Wedged between a wall and the front of a bus, he didn't know which way to move, as Glen only tried to push him out of the way.

"What you doing, Glen?" the staff member said. "Get off me, man!"

I look back on this moment, and it still cracks me up to think of two grown men fighting over an exit.

Later that night, we invited the MNPSG team to come out and check out this bus. We did and I tried to repeat our knocking question/answer process that worked earlier. Unfortunately, nothing came of it. No tappings. No knocks. No bathroom doors opening by themselves.

The crew did discover that the bathroom door actually has to open against gravity. It was startling to see because there was no way that just by Glen boarding the bus it would have been unlatched and swaying. The latch on the bathroom was even locked!

We had many more experiences that night at the Greyhound Bus Museum in Hibbing. One such experience led to the staff member making contact with something via our Cell Sensor EMF meter near the IR strobe. This would only happen when the Greyhound staff member was present; if a member of the MNPSG team tried to walk up to their location to watch, it would stop. I even tried sneaking up on the damn thing and it knew I was there!

What's odd about this (and we have this on video at our site) is that the staff member asked questions such as, "Are you the little girl people see?" and it answered yes. They even did a count up from one to see how old she was. It answered when the staff reached ten. They tried to go to eleven but they got no response until they went back down to ten.

Could they have made contact with the little girl seen roaming the grounds at Greyhound?

For me, the most startling part of the evening came when we were outside the museum. Glen had already set the alarm and left. Don was pulling out of the museum's parking lot. Mick and I were getting ready to leave. I just needed to dig my car keys out of my equipment box. Mick had his back to the museum's lobby doors and I noticed something that appeared to be a shadow around four feet tall walk from the bus room to the gift shop counter. I thought it was a trick of the lights and shrugged it off. I grabbed my keys and walked around the rear of my car. Mick had turned around and started to walk towards the museum's lobby doors.

"What's wrong? Please don't tell me you left something in there," I said with a disappointed tone.

"No…I didn't…I…just…" Mick tried to speak as his mind tried to rationalize what he just saw. "I thought I saw a shadow walk from the gift shop counter to the bus room. It was…well, do you know what an ewok is?"

(I knew what an ewok was; I'm a fan of the *Star Wars* movies. For those who do not know, they are the fuzzy little bears in *Return of the Jedi*.)

"That's the best way that I can describe that. It was like an ewok."

I told him what I had seen a few moments before he walked towards the museum. The hair on both of our arms stood straight up—we knew something was checking to see if it had full reign of the museum again.

Ever since 2009's excursions into the Greyhound Bus Museum, I have spoken at various seminars about the nights my team spent at the location; it is one of my favorites. I had no idea how much feedback I would receive from the general public on stories as well as their own encounters with the Little Ghost Girl of Third Avenue. I never knew how many peoples' lives this young girl affected.

From what I have been able to track down and learn about Hibbing, I believe the little girl was alive in the early 1900s, when Hibbing was a young pioneering town. Of course, Hibbing was not the Hibbing we know today. The town moved from its original location, which is now a Hibbing taconite mine pit called the Hull Rust Mahoning Mine Pit. The town moved in 1919 due to iron ore deposits found under the streets and was relocated to the nearby village of Alice. (To put it another way, Alice was wiped off the map and replaced by Hibbing.)

During my research on this legendary child, I found out that 1918 was not an easy year for Hibbing: the world was suffering through the Spanish Influenza epidemic. This town was not special nor protected against this disease, and a many people passed away, including children.

I spoke with many citizens of Hibbing about it. One gentleman who I met through the bus museum told me about his father recalling the 1918 Spanish Flu outbreak and how the town dealt with death. It was a very morbid back history—one that time has buried.

"My father used to tell us about the epidemic. Hibbing used to have an old Hupmobile that Mesaba Transportation donated for use that was all black. It was nicknamed 'the Black Mariah.' It was used to carry the dead to the cemetery and had a job much like a garbage truck; if a member of your family died, you put them on the curb to be picked up by the Black Mariah," he recalled in his story.

Oddly enough, the location that hosts the museum for Greyhound plays a large part in this gruesome history: the building sits on the land that was once used to hold the quarantine camp. After all, this was quite the prime location for the sick to stay in tents; when someone succumbed to the disease, it was an easy transport to the cemetery that borders the property to the south.

The Old North Hibbing Cemetery is quite an interesting spot of local history, and I believe it is heavily tied to the Little Ghost Girl of Third Avenue.

I have had the pleasure of seeing the original cemetery blueprints during my research, and I found out that though the cemetery was small, it was divided by a few different factors. The northern-most segment (the closest to Greyhound's museum) was reserved for children. South of them was where the Protestant adults were buried, and eventually a middle line was drawn that allowed the southernmost section to be used for Catholic adults (this would be the area near the water tower).

Unfortunately today, the cemetery is in neglect and some graves have been lost to the brush and trees in the western section. Some efforts have been made to restore these graves, but many citizens do not think it is worth the time.

As you can imagine, I experienced goose bumps to hear that children were buried along the property that borders the museum. In July of 2009, the MNPSG was lucky enough to encounter this child a few more times during our last time at Greyhound.

As you could probably tell, I am a big supporter of the museum (the ghosts are important to me, yes, but so is the historical significance), and I wanted to investigate the location one last time and share it with as many people as I could. I invited the local newspaper reporters (Matt N. and Mark), a college student doing a thesis paper (Becky), and the MNPSG's friends at the Northern Lights Paranormal Society (NLPS) in Grand Rapids (Johnny, Lisa, and Rick) to join us. This was the largest number of people outside of my own team I have ever invited to an investigation, and I did so because I knew Greyhound wouldn't let us down—it hadn't yet.

Almost the entire team of the MNPSG was present: Kristin, Mick, Don, Justin, and Matt R. came along. Glen was also with us for this night as our onsite staff representing the museum.

The interesting thing about working with another team is learning different methods, approaches, and equipment. The NLPS team brought along their own equipment, including a wireless audio system. Their team set up the wireless audio in the room with the numerous buses parked in it. After they were finished, we all broke into three teams and began scouring the property for any clues of this little girl.

She had fun with us that night.

The first odd thing that happened occurred in the northwest section of the Old North Hibbing Cemetery and was witnessed by Glen, myself, and the members of the NLPS. While filming some video, we had experienced what we thought was a dark shadow moving about the treeline to the west. We initially recorded this as a trick of the light on our eyes, but what others experienced that night led us to think differently.

A few hours later, the team consisting of Kristin, Mick, Justin, Mark, and Becky was on the walking trail that separates the cemetery from the museum. While recording EVP, they also reported seeing this shadow and hearing noises come from that section of the cemetery. When we reviewed the tape of their EVP session, the team had caught a little girl saying "HI!" very briefly and energetically.

It also appears that while we were outside later that night, this ghost girl was inside the museum causing a bit of a ruckus, growing weary of us being there. Around 1 a.m., the NLPS caught several audio files of a young (female) child crying and saying, "just leave us be!" We had no explanation for it, and because it was captured via a wireless audio system, I thought it could have been interference, like a baby monitor. The only problem with that is the fact that there aren't any residential houses within a few blocks of that part of town; I'm scratching my head about that one! (I should note that there is one apartment complex that hosts senior citizens on the south side of the cemetery, but I doubt they have or use baby monitors.)

Greyhound left quite an impression on many that night, and continues to do so to this day.

The following October, I was invited to do an educational seminar at the Hibbing Public Library and as always, this story started to twist more and more.

While setting up for the event, a family approached me and asked to talk to me. I always do my best to take time to listen to those who are brave enough to share their stories. One family member asked if I was the one who investigated the Greyhound Bus Origin Museum in town. I said yes, and she shared a story about her family's time at the museum's open house in May of 2009.

"We were at the Greyhound Museum's Open House this past spring. It's really an interesting building. My daughter had a little bit of a run-in there with a small ghost child. She said this girl tripped her. The problem is that when she told me about this, I don't remember seeing any children there other than her. She also said she saw a small ball rolling around the area by the bathrooms," she said with hesitation and confusion. "Does this make any sense to you?"

Now to be fair, I hadn't spoken a word about any real details about the ghost girl like I do today. That night was something that prompted me to write a feature story about the ghostly child. There were bits of information about the ghost girl from our investigations at the building, but there was very little put out there…certainly not enough for this lady to make up a story.

I was a bit shocked and confused because I hadn't expected to hear another story of this ghostly girl's antics. I didn't have much of an answer for her other than that, from what I'd heard, there was a ghostly girl said to roam Greyhound, so it was possible.

And with that, I began the seminar only to have this young girl come up again a few moments later after I started to talk about Greyhound and the police officers' experience.

"I know we've had some staff report problems with a ball mysteriously appearing and this girl being seen by my work as well," one lady reported. "I work on Howard Street, and I am not going to say where, but we have definitely seen her. A lot of us have!"

Dumbfounded and a bit taken aback, I stood there in silence. I mean what do you say other than, "Where do you work?"

Not many more answers came to me during that session, but it prompted me to share my experience on MinnesotaGhosts.com in the form of a feature article. I wanted to see if it caused more answers to come from the public. Unfortunately, not many did.

I put the ghost girl story on the back burner until the following year's seminar at the library. When I did this event in 2010, we had a really great crowd of people attend including the same family who experienced the ghostly girl at the Greyhound Bus Origin Museum's open house. I hoped to hear more about this ghostly girl and what she had been up to for the last year, but no one came forth during the seminar.

At the very end, however, I was approached by a father and son who came to me after the crowd shuffled out of the auditorium.

"You know that ghost girl that has been seen at the Greyhound?" the father asked.

"Yeah, what about her?" I said with a bit of skepticism.

"Well did you know how she travels around from location to location?"

"Uh…I heard she walks?" I replied with even more skepticism. I was tired and being a bit sarcastic as this man had a crazy look to him.

"No, she travels throughout town in a green ball of light. I've seen it. He's seen it," the man replied pointing to his son with enthusiasm and a smile.

"It comes out of the western part of the cemetery where all the graves are. This ball of light rises up around 1 a.m. and travels along the bike trail to Greyhound, the cemetery, and then southbound from there. If you want, I have an ATV that can get back there, and I'd be glad to show you sometime!"

His story made sense; in our last visit to Greyhound, we had our first experiences on the western border of the cemetery and then at the actual museum.

At this time, I have yet to take this stranger up on his offer but it certainly brings me more questions than answers. Just about the only thing I am sure of is that this is not going to be the last that I hear about this lost and lonely ghost girl who has made Third Avenue her home.

My conclusion on the Greyhound Bus Museum is that it is haunted by a variety of spirits who range from a little girl to possibly former mechanics or drivers. There may even be some people who have wandered in because they spent time on those buses while waiting to either go to war or return home. It is an interesting location very fond and dear to me.

16

THE MIGHTY SHIP

Growing up on the Iron Range, one of my favorite "vacation" spots was nearby Duluth and its Canal Park. An hour south of the Range, this location offers access to Lake Superior and many businesses that would not survive in my hometown.

While getting a summer tan, you might run across a mighty red ship docked in Canal Park named the *SS William A. Irvin*. This 600-foot ship has been docked in the harbor for the last twenty years after retirement from United States Steel (USS) Duty in 1978. It was a record-setting freighter for the line and a pioneer ship due to its technology and design.

The ship hosts a "Ship of Ghouls" attraction during the month of October where brave people can tour through the ship with costumed volunteers who try to scare them. The only problem is that sometimes something unknown rattles the costumed volunteers, which is how we were alerted to the ship, via Duluth Entertainment Convention Center (DECC) staff members.

We agreed to investigate the mighty ship in late November of 2009 with a team consisting of ten investigators to cover the 600-foot span of the freighter. This team consisted of Mickey, Don, Kristin, Matt R., Todd, Matt A., Michelle, Justin, Dave, and myself. The team would be broken up into three groups.

While on our tour, we were told about the death that had taken place on the ship, near the boiler room. A large pipe filled with steam and boiling water had broken and sprayed all over a ship worker, melting his skin. It is the only recorded death on the *Irvin*.

The staff did a wonderful job showing the team around but did not have any leads on activity or what historical event may have caused the paranormal activity on the ship. They only knew that staff members of the haunted attraction reported various experiences that stopped them from coming back to volunteer.

This was the first time our team would investigate a large vehicle; we were used to homes and museums. Having a limited power supply (as a ship does not have an electrical outlet every twenty feet) gave us an interesting challenge that took every inch of cord we had.

It was also interesting to investigate a well-known landmark in a nonoperational season; we received several calls from people asking if we knew there were people on board and that the ship's lights had been turned on.

The team broke into three groups and rotated around the ship. Team one consisted of Matt A., Todd, Kristin, and Matt R. Team two was Mickey, Justin, and Dave, and team three was Don, Michelle, and me.

At 9:00 p.m., team one investigated the wheelhouse and guest quarters. They reported nothing unusual other than walkie-talkie malfunctions and noises from the nearby trains.

At the same time, team two investigated the engine room and boiler room. In the boiler room, they noted that while investigating they asked for three loud knocks as a sign of a presence and received them. These knocks sounded like they came from the table in the crew dining quarters. When they rushed into the dining quarters, no one was there, and the sound of knocking on the table matched what they had heard.

Team three sat at command central and waited their turn to investigate.

At 10:30 p.m., the teams met at command central and switched positions. Team two investigated the wheelhouse and guest dining quarters. Team three investigated the crew dining quarters and engine room. Team one sat at command central.

While sitting in the crew dining quarters, team three reported seeing a shadow move across the mirror in the room. All three members saw it at the same time and reacted. Our cameras did not pick this up. The team separated and shared stories to see if they would be similar, rather than try to lead one another.

After this, team three investigated the boiler room and engine room. While in the engine room, Don mentioned seeing a shadow move across the door on the right-hand side of the boiler room. (This would have been the west side of the ship.) Our DVR cameras did not pick this up. It's interesting to note that while in the engine room later that night, Todd reported seeing something similar, not knowing about Don's report.

The teams regrouped at command central around 11:30 p.m. Team one investigated the engine room and boiler room. Adam and Michelle joined team two in investigating the captain's quarters and guest living quarters.

Michelle and Mickey sat in the captain's quarters while Adam, Justin, and Dave investigated the guest living quarters. Michelle and Mickey reported seeing a shadow move past a porthole but had no solid confirmation on this via equipment. Adam, Justin, and Dave did not report anything out of the ordinary in the guest living quarters.

At 12:15 a.m., the team started their equipment breakdown of the location to make good on our promise with the DECC to be off the ship by 1 a.m.

In reviewing our data from that night, we found a few oddities, including a sound file from our ambient audio recorder that was left in the engine room.

At approximately 10:10 p.m., a loud and violent shaking sound came across the recorder. This was about five minutes after team two had left the engine room after hearing the three strange knocks from the crew dining quarters.

Originally, we thought this could be the sound of the railings in the engine rooms shaking, but our DVR that was pointed at the brass railings did not show any type of movement.

While we do not know where this sound originated or what caused it, it is not enough for us to proclaim the ship haunted. Our team did have personal experiences onboard the ship during our time there, but we did not collect any solid, objective evidence to support the claim of a haunting.

In the year following the investigation, various people reached out to us via email. One letter stated that the sender's father used to work on the ship and had recently passed away around the time we were doing our investigation. He concluded that the activity we experienced that night might have been his father, since he used to work in the engine room and loved his duties aboard the ship. This was hard for us to verify, as we had no documented data or logic to base it on, but another letter made a lot of sense.

The letter came from a worker aboard another Great Lakes freighter. He said that the sound we recorded was very similar to the sound he experiences when his freighter is docked and then filled with ore pellets.

With the exception of the knocking we experienced in the dining quarters, this haunt very well could be residual, meaning that events from the past resonate in the present with no interaction with those who witness it. Experiences such as sounds and noninteractive visual stimuli are telltale signs of a residual haunting.

Since we were able to record a sound we never heard and never had any concrete interaction with the spirits that are said to roam the *SS William A. Irvin*, it appears that the past is repeating within the steel hull of the glorious freighter docked in Duluth's Canal Park.

17

A HEARTFELT CASE

I am often asked what advice I would give to people who want to do ghost hunting. There are three things I think everyone needs to understand about doing this that really don't come across in the television shows that spend so much effort "glamorizing" this field.

My first word of advice is that, like anything else you wish to be successful at in life, you have to dedicate your life to it. Just because I like to dance on the weekends doesn't mean I'm a professional backup dancer for Britney Spears.

The second piece of advice I have to give is whatever you do will eventually weave itself into you. People get known for what they do, and it becomes something people view as you. The greatest example is if you have ever had a family member be a professional plumber. If the toilet breaks, it is often that person who is called to come fix it, and it doesn't matter if they are on business hours or not.

My first taste of this came to me as a high school junior, while attending prom. A few other students thought it would be a fun thing to have the deejay play the song "Ghostbusters" by Ray Parker Junior. The only problem was that they replaced the chorus line following "Who ya gonna call?" with my own name. Not expecting this and unable to tell if this was a prank or a compliment, I was embarrassed, trying to live life as a normal teenager.

The third piece of advice I would give to anyone is that you should expect cases at times when you are not thinking about what stares back from the shadows. Much like the story about my high school prom, this happened to me during one of the biggest days of my life: my wedding.

While my wife and I made our rounds to thank our friends and family for attending the big event, we were stopped by a member of my family who told me they had a house for me to check out for ghosts. They explained the situation was for another member of my family whose parents owned the house; they were shaken up by the events that took place in the home.

A year prior to our wedding, a young lady named Sarah had passed away in the home after falling down a set of cement stairs. The authorities ruled it as an accident because she was drinking at the time. The family, however, didn't think it was that easy. The young lady who was killed was a previous girlfriend of their son, Travis, who had passed away in the home a few years before. He was found hanging in the basement in a suicide attempt.

The strange thing was that his ex-girlfriend had her fatal accident about five to seven feet from the spot where he was found.

Travis's family still owned the home and was thinking of selling it in an attempt to separate themselves from the terrible incidents they had experienced there. The only catch was that if we could make contact with either Travis or Sarah, they didn't want to sell the home because their loved ones were still there. They didn't want to abandon them.

Now, I should be a little clear on the fact that we never set out with the goal of verifying the person at the location for causing activity, because it is very rare that you are able to get clear answers to identify the entities. You rarely get a clear EVP or physical evidence saying that Joe Blow, who lived there sixty years ago and died in the house is the one causing the chandelier to swing. It just doesn't happen.

We agreed to check out the home and eventually did on January 30, 2010. The investigation team consisted of Mick, Matt A., Justin, and yours truly. Todd showed up at the investigation later that night.

As I drove to the small town of Eveleth where the home was located, the air was typical of a Minnesota winter: it was dry and cold. Walking outside felt like you were an astronaut without a helmet on. The roads were lined with small snowbanks on a very clear night where you could feel the stars shining. As I entered Eveleth, I followed the small convoy of cars leading us to the property. Matt A. was the convoy leader as he had known of the location. He was socially connected to Sarah, the ex-girlfriend of Travis.

We entered the home and were greeted by the members of Travis's family. I was related to the family through marriage, since Travis's sister had married one of my uncles. This was a hard case for me to handle because it was both personal to the family (since they wanted us to find out what happened to Travis), and members of my family were involved in this case. It is also generally hard to enter a case after a recent tragic event; most cases we handle have ghosts from eras more than fifteen years ago. This one would hit close to home no matter the outcome.

Per our team's protocol, we filmed just about every aspect of our investigations for two reasons. The first is that it allows us to remember things better, since locations are sometimes distracting and interesting. Secondly, it allows the public to peek into what we do and where we have been. After we film these sessions, the raw footage is archived for future reference (such as writing this book or if we experience a case like it down the road) and it is also edited down to a shorter version for our website, MinnesotaGhosts.com.

During our filming, we asked the clients the back history of the home. Travis's mother gave us a brief tour of the home. We asked her to tell us what alleged paranormal experiences had happened in the home so we would know where to focus our attention.

We learned that the home had been in the family for some time. Travis's parents used to live in the home before moving and passing it along to their children. The home was not original to the property; it was moved to its current location after a local mining company had found iron ore under the small village where it used to be.

During our interview with Travis's parents, his father had told us that there were a few odd things he noticed while living in the home but never really thought twice about. He would often hear walking upstairs when no one was home. He attributed this to the house adjusting to Minnesota's ever-changing climate. However, he couldn't explain the battery-operated toys in the kids' room turning on all on their own. In one instance, he entered the playroom looking for a toy and when he couldn't find it, he gave up the search. Upon exiting the room, he heard the toy say, "Goodbye! Goodbye!" Perhaps too scared to find his own answer, he had no explanation for that experience.

When their son, Mark, lived in the home after Travis's passing, he claimed to see little girls in the dining room on the first floor, and when he went to investigate as to who they were, he would find no one. Another startling claim that came from him was that when he was sleeping on the couch in the living room, he would be woken up by the feeling of something cold wrapping around his neck.

The first stories the family had heard of Sarah's spirit being in the home came from Mark shortly after her accident in the home. He claims that he still sees her in the home and had a conversation with her once.

Before our visit, Mark had a scare with an overdose. He told his family that his addiction became stronger while in the home, and due to the experiences and temptations he believed the house had provided him, the family said Mark does his best to avoid the property.

While in the basement, Travis's mother told us about that section of the home being a gathering place for the friends and family who visited. It had easy access to the outside and was a spot where they would often gather to talk to Travis after his passing. The spot in which he took his life was not very far away, and Sarah was said to frequent the spot to have conversations with him.

Travis's parents told us that a new tenant had started to live in the home, and we were able to meet him during our interview. This new resident was a friend of the family and had agreed to take in Travis's old dog, a pit bull.

While in the home, the dog would react to things as if someone was talking to him. He would show excitement and fear as if being yelled at. This was startling to the family because the dog only exhibited this behavior within the home. The family found it odd, since he was disconnected to many people after Travis's passing.

They also mentioned that the dog had a fear of going into the kitchen and would often stop at the threshold of the dining room and kitchen. The two rooms did have different types of flooring; the kitchen was linoleum and the dining room was carpet. I am not sure if this was responsible for the dog's reaction; some have a hard time with linoleum flooring.

After hearing much of the history of the home, I had to ask if they had ever used a Ouija board in the home. This may seem a bit cliché and is not something I normally ask but here is why I did: the home had some very negative effects on people within the building.

In the course of about two years, the activity had ramped up to a climax, and there were dire consequences for those in the home for a prolonged period of time. One resident had attempted suicide twice and only within the home. Another resident had tried to kill himself with drugs and claimed that while in the home, he heard voices telling him to kill himself. A frequent visitor who had ties to the home passed away in an "accident." Two incidents happened within ten feet of each other.

Something was wrong with this house, and my past experiences told me that ghosts do not do foul things like this. In all my time dealing with ghosts, I find them to be the same as they were in life. Some are good, some are bad, but most are confused and looking for answers just as we all do in life. Very few attempt to do harm on a regular basis. Something in that house was feeding off fear and abuse—never a good thing to find on a case.

Responding to my question about the Ouija board, the people in the room reacted as memories flashed back into their heads. Travis's dad claimed there had been one in the home, but he wasn't sure if it ever had been used.

Travis's sister had the answer to that question: she assured her dad that one *had* been used in the home before. Her mom was also positive one was used because the two had used it together in the room that was once the children's playroom; the room in which the toys had started acting up.

One thing I wish I could put on a billboard and devote a paid-for television commercial to is that a Ouija board is not just a game. They are a communication device. Have you ever accidently called a wrong number or pocket-dialed a strange number and felt fearful that you didn't want whoever was on the other end to be rude or mad at you? Maybe you just didn't want to talk to a strange person? The board is almost the same thing; you do not know who is on the other end of the line, so you don't want to attract attention to the original caller.

Most people use a Ouija board in hopes of contacting a loved one who has passed, or they are just curious to see what will happen. If you are thinking of using a

Ouija board for the first reason, it isn't worth it. From my time with ghosts, I have yet to meet one who has told me through EVP that they were the ones who interacted with the residents through a board. If you are a person with the second reason, please understand that I am passing this family's experience along to you as an example of what happens.

Unfortunately, there are things that lurk in the dark that are not ghosts. It may sound like a scare tactic but it's not. One thing to realize is that at one point in time, ghosts were human. There are things out there that never were human. You can call these things whatever you wish—demons, angels, faeries, tulpas, etc.—but just remember that many do not like humans. As an investigator, I do not like to empower these entities by calling them by name or even saying they are a "demon" because, at the end of the day, they are just inhuman. Many wish that they were once human, and in the eyes of some religious folks, they are jealous that humans received God's favor. (Note: I try to stay away from religious stereotypes as much as possible because there is too much conflict in belief when talking to the public.)

Learning that a Ouija board was used in the home-made me a bit unnerved, to be quite honest. I had only worked on one case prior that dealt with an inhuman entity. These cases sometimes seem unaffected by what we do and can turn into nasty experiences. I had brought a relatively new team to this type of encounter and had to put myself on the front line to help protect them. I had no time to teach them what to expect or do. After all, they were used to looking for ghosts, which is much like greeting a stranger in the supermarket. If I had to create a metaphor for meeting this type of entity, let's say I was like Clarice Starling in *Silence of the Lambs*.

And on top of all of this, I was still supposed to see if the spirits of Travis and Sarah were present in the home. As mentioned before, it is hard and rare to get an identity from a particular spirit.

This was going to be a hard night.

We finished setting up our equipment and getting the team familiar with the layout of the house. The family had left at this point to "do whatever [we] needed to do." The first part of the night was relatively quiet, which in all honesty unnerved me more. We were on the clock to get some type of evidence to present to the client that supported their claims, and we also wanted (hopefully) to bring them peace of mind about their son. I was also worried about the first activity being a "snap rather than a ramp." By this, I mean that the first activity was going to be something extreme rather than the activity powering up as time went on. In cases like this, we are more likely to have someone get hurt by either a physical reaction from an entity or getting scared and causing harm personally while reacting.

Luckily for us, we didn't get the snap.

Our first piece of evidence came after two hours of investigating; I was watching the DVR unit while Mick and Justin were checking out the master bedroom upstairs. There was a light anomaly on the screen that I thought might be from a flashlight or reflection. At the first available opportunity, I went upstairs to try to recreate what I had seen with the equipment the team had up there. There were a few mirrors in the room, but nothing was able to recreate what we had captured. I am still not sure what it was, and to this day, it is still something that makes me scratch my head. It is unlike anything else I have ever seen with ghosts, so I am not even sure in saying it was created by ghosts.

This little light source hovered near the door handle, growing in intensity and luminosity. It was also between the camera and the door rather than being on the door like a normal shadow or reflection would be. I learned this when Justin passed in front of our camera: it showed up on his leg rather than the room's door. Put quite simply, it was bizarre.

While we were in a smaller bedroom on the second floor, the second odd thing came to our team. This was the room in which Travis had first attempted suicide. The room was in shambles, debris was strewn about and a bed (simply a bare mattress on a wooden frame) was angled in the middle of the room. It was clear that no one used this room.

I was in this room while Matt A. was in the second smaller bedroom and Todd, who had showed up after our initial setup, was in the master bedroom. We all decided to sit in these separate rooms and listen for anything abnormal.

While taking readings with a Mel Meter, I noticed an abnormal EMF spike on the center of the bed. After playing around with the meter in different spots throughout the room, I called the other two investigators to my location. I wanted their take on the situation and to see if having more witnesses would change the data. (Believe it or not, some entities do get "stage fright" with a larger audience, and activity will drop off with more people.)

We spent twenty minutes trying to figure out why the center of this bed had a 4.5 mG (milligauss) reading and the sections around the bed read below 1 mG. I was stumped and had no explanation, so I did the best thing I could think of; I started to ask questions. As I started to ask, Todd and Matt returned to their listening spots.

With video rolling on the device, I started to explain that whatever was in the room with me could touch the device on the bed and make the numbers change. I asked first to move from a 3.5 reading to a 4.0. It did! So naturally, I asked it to go higher in case it was a fluke.

"Can you make it go to a 5.0?" I asked. The device went up to a 5. In case something wanted to speak, I decided to place a digital audio recorder next to the bed. When I did this, the reading dropped back to a 3.0.

I was fairly certain something was intelligent enough to respond to me so I decided to ask if its name was Travis or Sarah with the audio on the video camera and the audio recorder capturing sound. Since I couldn't hear what was being recorded, I only had the Mel Meter's digital reading display to interact with, so I continued to stick to the numbers. As I asked more questions, the numbers continued to flux. When I stopped asking questions, the device numbers stayed the same.

The highest reading we received was a 6.6 mG. Before we jump to conclusions, I do want to mention that I did not associate this with being an inhuman entity, even though it was close to what some consider the "mark of the beast."

Oddly enough, towards the end of my session, I heard a voice coming from the master bedroom, where Todd was. I thought the sound was one of the two investigators, so I cut my session short to see what they needed. When I went to talk to both of them about what they needed, neither claimed to have said a word, but Todd mentioned that his EMF meter registered a spike.

Did something approach him and enter the room he was in?

We decided to leave a DVR camera on the Mel Meter in the room I conducted my session to record if there was any change between having a person in the room or not. Our conclusion from that night showed that the meter registered a higher milligauss reading when someone was in the room asking questions. The baseline reading was a 3.0 to 3.5 mG with no one in there; 4.0 to 5.3 mG with someone in there, and a maximum of 6.6 mG when someone asked questions. I have no logical explanation for this test data.

Towards the end part of the night, Mick received a startle. He was investigating the master bedroom with Todd and Justin. They were asking questions with very little response. Being curious and also in the dark, Mick reached for a book that was on a nightstand. When his hand touched the cover of the book, two EMF meters spiked. One of the devices we use is the Cell Sensor model, which has an audible alarm for an increase in EMF and a red light that illuminates; the higher the EMF signal, the more intense the alarm and light.

A bit shocked, Mick put down the book and both EMFs went back to normal. As always, we believe things are a coincidence and repeat actions that provide data. He picked up the book and the EMFs spiked again. Mick turned on his head lamp to see what book was causing this to happen—it was the Bible.

Unaware of what was going on; I was talking to Matt A. downstairs with a video camera recording our conversation. Matt had known Sarah in life, and we were talking about her circumstances regarding the accident in the basement when my walkie chirped. It was Mick asking me in a calm fashion to come upstairs because he didn't understand what was going on.

With camera rolling, I went upstairs to check on the team. My whole night was quiet, which I was thankful for, but knowing that we could be dealing with an inhuman entity was always in the back of my head. I was nervous for my team's safety as well as the family.

Mick explained to me what they were doing and proceeded to show me. Just as before, as soon as his fingertips touched the cover of the book, the meters sounded and lit up.

This was a moment when I'd had enough of this case and had seen enough of the evidence to know what we were dealing with. It was clearly an inhuman entity case causing trauma to feed off the emotions that the tragic events in the house produced. I decided to gather up my team and pull out every trick I had learned to deal with this situation.

I will admit that I am not a demonologist and do not have the proper training to handle these cases on a regular basis. I don't recommend that anyone go out looking for these evil inhuman entities. I was stuck in a pickle with this case and had to get out of my own comfort zone to attempt to remedy this situation, even if only temporarily.

As mentioned previously, I only know a bit about the psychic and the demonology fields. But I do have an "in case of emergency" list that a few friends have taught me in case I ever found myself in a situation like I did with this case.

I rounded up the team and told them that we were going to be starting our wrap-up soon. We would first start to break down the equipment and go about our business as if we found nothing in the home. After this was done, we would go into the rooms where we had experienced activity and say a prayer.

When this was done, we would leave the home as if nothing had happened there. We acted like nothing happened so we didn't give the possible entity what it wanted which was fear.

When we were done gathering our equipment, we went into the two bedrooms upstairs that we had experienced activity and recited the Lord's Prayer in each room. As someone who is not religious, this is one of the few things I know about, and it was the first time that many on my team had experienced doing something religious in an investigative setting. While my team was reciting the prayer, I did something I learned from a trusted psychic, Echo Bodine.

One thing Echo had taught me is that there is a higher set of beings that exist within our realm called "the Squadron." Being religious herself, Echo describes this unit as an angelic special forces. At any time you feel unsafe around a negative entity, you can ask for help from "the Squadron" to clear out the property and assist removing these entities.

I wasn't sure how much it would work, but I figured I didn't have many other options. I decided to try calling "the Squadron" while we were in the basement. I chose this location because there was so much emotion and energy stored there from the two fatal events. If there was any place within the home this thing was storing up energy, it would have been in this location.

After attempting to clear the home, the team left and we all had safe travels to our homes. In the coming days, we reviewed the evidence and prepared it for the client. We were still hoping we would find a small sliver of evidence that we had made contact with the deceased loved ones so the family could have some closure and find healing.

We had one audio file from the basement area that sounded like voices talking. We are certain it was not anyone on our team, as it was recorded prior to us entering the basement and was picked up on an ambient recorder. It was unclear what the voices said, but the family would later be convinced it belonged to Travis.

Is he still in the home looking over the family? It could be possible; I have no evidence to say that he isn't. However, we didn't gather enough to affirm he was still there, either. Sometimes the evidence is not so much what you think as it is what the client thinks.

In talking with the family, things have been quieter in the home, and they feel a bit more at ease.

This case is one I am often asked about by people in the area because both Travis and Sarah were remembered kindly by the community. It's not easy to say that this case is closed because it had so much tragedy within it; very little closure came from our investigation.

Sometimes we forget that these cases aren't so much black or white, but rather various shades of gray.

18

DON'T RUN AWAY

One of my true pleasures in doing paranormal research is the somber tone of a cemetery at night. As one can imagine, it is a different world most are scared to enter. However, if one is brave enough to accept what might be encountered; it can be a phenomenal time and a moment that can truly stir up some heartfelt emotions. For me, it is a time to reflect and let the ever-busy world calm down.

When I lived in Mankato, I did a lot of historical research in cemeteries during the day because the area had a vast sea of significance within the state's history. At night, I spent a lot of time trying to find myself as well as trying to see what could be seen that the daylight hid.

I remember one such occasion within Mankato's Glenwood Cemetery in 2005 that still sends chills up my spine.

One humid summer night, a friend asked me to take him to a cemetery so he could see what this "ghost hunting business" was all about. I normally do not do this, but since I had decided I wanted to get out and experience the night life, we decided to go.

After parking our cars, we loaded our gear by flashlight. I normally grab a digital recorder for audio and maybe a digital still camera. (Video cameras do not shoot far enough in outdoor locations for any significant video to be captured.) We put on a headlamp each and ventured into the raccoon-infested resting spot. (Seriously, it was a spooky place and a first where I've had a million eyes staring back from the darkness, like in a cartoon.)

As we began our power walk through the cemetery, I stopped to point out a few historical markers like I normally do to add educational value and to respect the deceased. There are a few famous Minnesotans within that cemetery, including the Sibley family and the famous author Maud Hart Lovelace.

As we came upon the large shed the groundskeepers use for various projects, I noticed a small boy standing on the asphalt pathway. He was in a newspaper boy cap, tweed coat, but more importantly he was missing his legs. He looked translucent with a slight hint of blue, not illuminating but he had a slight glow to him. More incredibly, he was looking at my friend and I walking towards him.

I put my arm out to stop my friend as the sound of our feet crunching gravel came to a stop.

"Do you see that?" I asked, not wanting to tell him what I saw so he could verify what I was seeing myself.

"No, I don't. What are we looking at?" he replied.

I stared at this ghost boy for a few more minutes, and it seemed like an eternity. I then decided that we needed to do something to break this moment so I started to walk towards the young transparent boy. Going back to my Ghostbusters fandom in my head, I realized this was my "library moment" and one can hope that the outcome came out better than the movie's scene.

Panic set in, and the young ghost lad darted off to the side of the shed. Right then, I forgot the strangeness of the scenario and treated it like chasing any young boy with a pulse. I ran after him and tried to stop him.

As with any chase, my target became lost. I was baffled but I knew I shouldn't be. I spun around the area where I lost track of the apparition as my friend caught up. He was naturally asking me why I decided to run in a dark cemetery, and more importantly, leave him behind. I told him what I saw and why I darted off in a hurry. He was a bit unnerved at this point.

I had looked all around for any sign of the boy but never bothered to look down at the markers. I asked my friend to help me look at the foot markers, now curious about where we were. I feared this would eventually be one of those moments where everything made sense and ended up in a book because the ending to this tale was too perfect.

I was right.

We were standing in the children's section of the cemetery, most dates ended in the 1920s.

19

THE HOUSE
THAT PALMER BUILT

Nestled quietly within Main Street America's culture in a
small town in central Minnesota is a brick building that
holds many secrets within its walls. This place was the
first to be built in the quaint town of Sauk Centre, Minnesota, and at one time boasted being the first hotel outside the Twin Cities area to have electricity; it was such
a novelty in those days, people literally booked rooms to
play with the light switches and marvel at their efficiency.

Strange? You don't know the half of it!

This hotel was also the working place of a famous author named Sinclair Lewis who went on to chronicle life

175

in his hometown in books such as *Main Street* and *Babbitt*. The people of this hotel were his character fodder when he was a bellhop, and his daily chores were always getting in the way of his writing genius; so much that he would often sneak down to the basement to scribe new ideas and things he had witnessed.

The location I am referring to is called the Palmer House Hotel. It was one of the places on my bucket list—and it only took me roughly six years to get there.

The hotel is so steeped in history that I could not do it justice here about all the important people who have stayed in its rooms, nor could I begin to tell you of all the strange reports that have been documented from the countless paranormal investigations that have been conducted here.

All I can do is tell you my story and how I came to fall in love with the Palmer House Hotel and the time-warped essence within the walls of this establishment.

When I began my journey to find answers about my uncle and how to say goodbye, it was a personal mission. Through this adventure I have found others who are just as genuinely interested in personal discoveries as myself, which you have no doubt read about in earlier chapters. You may have even read my reasons for starting MinnesotaGhosts.com and why I wanted it to be an online database people could research that told the honest truth about locations and the deep albeit weird history of Minnesota.

I never thought my passion would result in places requesting my presence. The Palmer House Hotel was one of those places.

I became familiar with Kelley Freese, the owner and proprietor of the hotel, around 2005. I don't remember how we first met or how we got to talking, but we're still in touch today, and I am thankful for it. Ever since we met, we have discussed the goings-on at the haunted inn in great detail via email and over the phone. We have consulted with each other about the happenings at her business, events that pertain to para-entertainment, and teams that have requested to investigate the Palmer House Hotel.

For further clarification about the team aspect of our consultations, I should mention that I do my best to research each and every team that investigates hauntings in the state of Minnesota. I do this mainly for one reason: I pass cases that are out of my reach to others who conduct themselves in a manner much like my team. This is something that I have believed in for years and one reason why I believe in and am involved with the TAPS family.

During our many conversations, Kelley always brought up my needing to make a trek to the infamous haunt others are literally scratching on the door to get into. I always wanted to but never could find the time, which was a shame because I felt like I knew more about the place than my own home.

In 2008, I was running the MNPSG with two chapter teams; one in northern Minnesota and one in Mankato. It was this November when the Mankato team decided to take Kelley up on her offer and check into the hotel.

I am glad they did.

After reviewing the evidence from that night, they found a bizarre piece of video footage that still has me puzzled to this day. Since I was leading the northern team, I missed this grand opportunity but was lucky enough to watch the video.

The team had set up a digital video recorder's infrared camera on top of a shelving display unit. The camera was facing into the pub area through two French doors. At around 3 a.m., the video reveals a human figure step out of the shadows and into the light coming in from a window. It appears to look into the French doors, notice the camera, and then return from whence it came. The oddest part of this footage is that when whatever it is disappears, it also seems to vaporize as it moves away.

Since the day I experienced this video, I have challenged each and every team I know personally to visit the Palmer House Hotel and recreate this video. Many have tried (including myself) but have yet to get close to an answer.

A few years later, in March of 2010, I finally visited the Palmer House Hotel; the MNPSG was invited to check it out with our own equipment once again. Spring was slowly taking hold in Minnesota as the weather turned and the landscape thawed. I was excited, of course, and the weather was definitely multiplying that feeling for me.

It was around 4 p.m. when we arrived in Sauk Centre. I found myself staring at the antique neon sign that defines the exterior of the Palmer House Hotel—I had arrived at my *Titanic*.

I use that phrase because I felt like I could relate to all the historians who studied the famous ship and got to know its history and beauty well but had never set foot aboard it. I suppose I had the upper hand because I was still able to experience the Palmer House Hotel. For the first few hours, I was mystified, putting together all the puzzle pieces of all the physical décor that makes the Palmer House Hotel so unique. Until that time, I had seen it all through various videos and photographs.

We arrived at the hotel on a quiet day. The team I had brought consisted of Dave, Justin, Kristin, and myself.

I walked into the pub area and found Kelley sitting at the bar, conversing with a patron of the establishment. When I entered the room, she bounced up from her stool and let her large smile speak her excitement.

You could tell from how she dressed that she was a very down-to-earth woman. She had an intellectual look with her rectangular glasses but showcased a blue-collar attitude with jeans and a zip-up hooded sweatshirt. As she spoke with us, she used a large stainless steel coffee tumbler as if it were an extension of herself. Despite just meeting a group of strangers, she was comfortable and you could tell she was at home within the hotel.

As we began to carry in our bags of equipment, Kelley invited us to take a look around and let her know which rooms we would like. She mentioned that all the rooms were available except for one as it was booked by a family. She invited me to show the team around the hotel because she believed I knew just about as much about the location as she did.

The team climbed to the third floor and began our walk down the corridor to rooms 17 and 22. On our way there, I told the team a bit about the rooms' history.

"A young lady named Lucy is believed to occupy room 17. She was thought to be a lady of the night during the early days of the hotel when it was the Sauk Centre House. She was killed by her pimp, a man named Raymond, and if you sit in both chairs in Lucy's room, you leave her with no choice but to sit on the bed. Given her occupation, the bed makes her pretty uncomfortable," I mentioned to the team as we walked.

"What's with room 22 then?" asked Dave.

"Well room 22 coincides with Lucy's room which is directly across the hall," I answered. "Room 17 is considered to be Raymond's room, and it is a place where women report feeling uncomfortable. Which room do you want, Dave?"

"I'll take Raymond's room," Dave said with a smile.

"Okay, great, because I wanted to give Justin (who had yet to arrive) the opportunity to be in Lucy's room," I explained. I decided to do this for Justin because he is often the most anxious and willing team member; Lucy's room is the most requested room in the hotel. It was a perfect fit!

As we stepped back into the hallway between the rooms, I noticed a small black shadow drag down the steps near the landing. Naturally, I became curious and went to see if something had fallen off a ledge or chair. To me, it appeared to be something made of cloth. As I approached the landing, I noticed that nothing was wrong, and my team became curious as to why I stopped talking and rushed over to the staircase.

"I just thought I saw something go down the stairs," I said with a hesitant tone as I tried to piece together a solution. "It looked as if it was a train from a wedding dress getting pulled down the stairs but it was dark, not white."

With no explanation for what I had witnessed, we left it at just something odd and noted it for later. I had never heard of any stories about a woman in a dress near the staircase, so this was definitely not fitting with what I knew about the hotel.

Once Justin arrived, we told him about his opportunity to stay in Lucy's room—he was ecstatic. Dave jokingly mentioned to him not to worry because if he had to scream and run out, he could certainly take harbor in Dave's room, which was just across the hall. Justin smiled at Dave nervously because he did not know exactly what went on in the room he was going to sleep in, as he missed the room picking situation.

We filmed our tour of the Palmer House Hotel (as we do in all tours) for viewers on our website so they could get a first-hand look at our tour with the client. Kelley did a great job, and while we were in room 17, Lucy's room, she told us about how the door is known to shut. While talking about this, the door shut on me and hit me in the shoulder. I was staring through the LCD screen in my camera, and no one was around me. Like always, I tried to recreate the action by stamping my feet on the carpet, but no such luck. Were these all inklings of things to come later that night?

When we began our investigation that night, we decided to try something called a "Shack Hack" in the hotel's basement area. A Shack Hack is basically a broken radio set to permanently scan radio waves; the theory is that the spirits can make random words from the noise generated. We had seen others use it at the Palmer House Hotel and figured we would give it a shot. We never believed in it until that night.

While in the basement, we decided to "go dark," meaning we were in complete darkness with only bits of ambient light from the stairwell. After we started our session, we filmed for our own documentation. Soon enough, we started to get weird words such as my own name being called out. This was unusual to me but not to the Palmer House

Hotel—another good friend of mine has had her own name called out in the same location through the same device.

As the Shack Hack continued its work, I noticed in the ambient light from the stairs that something was pacing in front of the door we had walked through. As I started to watch this, the device started to say very odd and negative things like, "Get out," "kill," and "die." Whatever positive voices that were there before seemed to be leaving, and this new voice frightened me. For the safety of the team, I decided to end this session and leave the basement.

When we walked past the area where I had seen the pacing, the entire team instantly noticed a strong sulfur smell they found quite repulsive. Oddly enough, the odor only occurred in this doorway.

After our experience in the basement, I decided it would be better for the team to stay out of there for a few hours and let whatever was down there calm a bit. While investigating the lobby area between the staircase and the pub area, Kristin and I heard a very sharp dog-like bark come from the top of the basement steps area. After hearing it, I communicated with Dave and Justin via our walkie-talkies and found that at the moment we heard the bark, they were researching what Native Americans call a "pukwudgie," a small human-like spirit (much like a troll) that lives in unfinished and cluttered areas and sometimes makes dog-like noises and produces strong foul smells. While doing preliminary research on the property, we found that this Native American entity was said to have ties to the location. Originally, we thought it would be a farfetched idea, as we deal with ghosts, not imaginary troll-like spirits.

After finding out about this strange "coincidence" of hearing a dog bark and having my team read that very same passage about the thing in the basement at the same time, I decided to give the basement one more shot. We had watched a video produced by others that showed what another investigator called "rushing," when the black masses in the basement block out the light by approaching humans and creating a dark shadow on infrared cameras. I rounded up Justin and we headed down to conduct one more Shack Hack experiment.

While in the basement, we began hearing similar results as before, with one very harrowing word come through the box. This is what made me a true believer in the box, because the word that came across is very rare but one that fit the situation very well: "pukwudgie."

After hearing this come across, I knew I was beyond my usual ghost hunting field and into something a bit darker and much more serious. Even Native American shamans avoid this type of spirit, so I knew I was in over my head. For the rest of the night, I decided it was for the best that the team stuck to the levels above the basement. It was not so much fear of the entity as it was a rule of respect. In this field, you need to walk fine lines and pick your battles.

In my time learning about the Palmer House Hotel, I have heard a lot about the hours between 3 a.m. and 4 a.m. This is when the ghosts of the Palmer House really are said to act up on the lobby levels and above. After all, this time period is when our November 2008 video with the shadow figure was filmed, so it was a great chance for us to see with our own eyes what the camera saw. We decided to separate and watch the lobby area.

While doing so, we began hearing very unexplainable things. The first thing I heard was the sound of a young boy singing the song "Alouette" from the staircase. This sounded like it was coming from either the second or third floor. Besides a family sleeping on the other side of the hotel, we were alone in the building! I asked the rest of the team to listen and see if they could hear it, but no one else said they were able to hear it. I decided to sit there and watch the staircase, and a few moments later I saw a black mass wrap around the staircase and disappear as if it were peeking to see what we were doing.

Thinking back about the staircase, a psychic once told the owner that the ghost of a young boy likes to play on the staircase. Some local history has even suggested that a young boy fell and died on the stairs there. This finding was led by the various stories of young children saying they don't want to leave the hotel while their parents check out at the front desk because they want to stay and play with the young boy.

Around 3:18 a.m., I heard a sound that was both un-explainable at the time and something another person on my team heard. Dave first asked me if I heard the chiming of what sounded like a clock or a music box. It was not a simple chime but rather a melody. Originally we thought it was something in the dining room area and decided to look around for a clock. Looking around, we found a clock hanging on the wall and decided this was it and forgot about it. We had found the natural explanation for the sound.

As we sat in the lobby and listened for some other oddities, we heard this melody play again from a different part of the hotel around 3:35 a.m. I started to question the clock theory a bit more and looked back on when the chiming first began. This sound could not have been something outside like a church clock because it was not ringing on the hour or even at a steady rate of, say, every fifteen minutes. I spoke to Dave about it, and he estimated that he had first heard it when I heard the boy singing "Alouette" on the staircase, which was shortly after 3 a.m.

While Dave and I were figuring this out, we noticed that the rest of the team was starting to fall asleep, so I decided to pull the plug on our night investigation and wrap up the equipment. Since there was a family in the hotel, we didn't want to inconvenience them by leaving our equipment up, so we broke it all down and made it to bed around 4:30 a.m.

My wife and I checked into room 11. I stayed awake a bit and watched TV. As I laid there and watched the small television with *The Fresh Prince of Bel-Air* on, I noticed that the top left corner of the screen started to turn black and white and go fuzzy as if something was interfering with the TV. It only lasted a few seconds and then went back to normal. I made note of it because the rest of the picture was unaffected. This happened maybe a total of two or three times during a ten-minute segment.

I eventually fell asleep around 5:30 a.m. and was woken up around 6 by what felt like a feather brushing my nose. I quickly jerked awake and saw two black dots on the white wall. They hovered at bed level for a few seconds and then quickly jerked upwards and faded away. It was odd because they were dark and not like a normal "eye spot" that seems to cycle colors. It almost felt like someone was crouching next to me and then when it saw I was awake, got up and left.

I naturally was a bit startled and woke up my wife. She was a bit unnerved and didn't sleep after hearing this. I knew I needed more sleep for the four hour drive home, so I continued to try to get more rest.

A little after 7 a.m., I was woken to the sounds of what appeared to be crying coming from our bathroom. It sounded like a female sobbing into a cloth. I thought it was Kristin, so I got up and rolled over, only to find her sitting beside me watching television. I asked her if she heard the sobbing and she said no. I got up, went into the bathroom, and it stopped. By this point, I felt like I was in an episode of *The Twilight Zone* and questioning my own sanity.

By 7:30, the rest of the living guests were awake and starting to make a bit of commotion in the hallways. I figured it was time to make a day of it and head downstairs for breakfast, where we met with Dave. I asked him if anything strange happened to him during the night; he said no. Continuing to breakfast, we waited for Kelley to arrive and for Justin to wake up.

After our meal, I decided to go check the ghost logs from past visitors and compare notes. While doing so, Kelley walked into the hotel and was eager to find out what the team had experienced during the night. We shared our stories from the previous night, including the story about the chiming.

Kelley brought us into the dining room and showed us the clock that we thought we heard during the night. She explained that it was something she had on showcase from a local artisan and hotel guests could actually buy one. She hit the demo button on the side of the clock and the entire face separated and moved about while playing a much different tone than we had heard during the night. This was not the same clock! Kelley then explained that this clock had a solar panel in it that prevented it from playing during the night, when most people were asleep.

While we were watching the clock demo, Justin came downstairs. We asked how his night was, and he said that he had gotten sleep and was uninterrupted despite hearing one odd thing he didn't understand.

During the night, he had heard something dragging across the carpet in his room. He thought it was a piece of his luggage, so he said out loud with his eyes shut, "Please, I am tired, and you can take anything but the laptop." The noise stopped.

We talked with Kelley for about two hours afterwards about the experiences that night before we left. She was quite interested in all we had experienced within the building. Her situation is unique; she is able to relive a familiar location through the eyes of newcomers. I still talk to Kelley quite regularly, and things are just as active at the hotel. Most recently, close to New Year's Eve of 2012, a patron was called and informed that their dinner reservation was being cancelled. The only problem is that no living staff member called to cancel, but the caller ID showed the hotel's number!

The Palmer House Hotel is definitely haunted and one of the most active spots I have ever visited in my twelve-year history of doing investigations. I would have no problem venturing back to revisit the things that approached me and my team that March. While I had originally gone there wanting to find an answer to that shadow video, I came back with many more questions about the hotel in general.

I look forward to many more adventures in Sauk Centre in the years to come.

20

THE UNEXPECTED VISITOR

During my time in the field, I have run into many individuals with different backgrounds and reasons for getting involved in paranormal research. Some of these people consider it a "calling," and others just happen to get involved due to interest from curiosity.

Due to the little things in life, such as the birthday cake with the ghosts on it, I would happen to be one of those people who think of it as a calling.

People always think what I do consists of smooth sailing moments where we get to waltz into haunted locations, talk to the spirits, gather evidence of them being there, and move on to the next location.

However, there are always bumps along the road that make me wish that I never got involved in the paranormal. Over the course of my time ghost hunting, I have asked myself several times, "Why do I continue to do this?" I don't get paid for it, I receive a lot of shit for it, and it affects what could ultimately be the normal life of a mortgage, kids, and a career.

My "calling" affects both my personal and public lives. Many personal moments have allowed me very unique and rewarding experiences due to my talents. Moments like those are quite valuable.

Likewise, I have had negative moments in my life where I have been adversely affected by the course that I took with my life. Since I do not make a living from my dealings with ghosts, I have to find ways to support myself elsewhere. These jobs usually mean working with others, and sometimes I meet people who don't believe in ghosts. I remember one job in particular where a supervisor said I was "always out late at night chasing around spooks as a Ghostbuster" in response to my quitting. Actually, I quit because I felt bored at the job and was unhappy.

One person whose work I have followed for years is John Zaffis, a paranormal and occult researcher in New England. John has written many books, collaborated with various paranormal movies and documentaries, and is a relative of

Ed and Lorraine Warren. The Warrens were the investigators in the famously infamous Amityville Horror case.

When he was first getting started in his own "line of work," John followed his relatives around on cases, observing what they did and how they did it. In his book, *Shadows of the Dark*, he writes about how they did not allow him to join them until he was eighteen years old because "the work" was too much. When John finally turned eighteen, Ed took him into a room and sat him down. John shares what Ed said to him at that moment: "I want you to realize something—once you've been touched by the supernatural and once you get involved, your life will never be the same."

I appreciated this phrase because it echoes heavily in my own life. My life has been filled with odd, frightening, and macabre experiences. However, it also has been insightful, unique, and adventurous.

So what keeps driving someone to push down this "spooky yellow brick road?" For me, it all comes down to one experience I had in 2005.

After some time at Mankato State University, I decided college wasn't right for me at that time. I made the tough decision to drop out. About a year later, I was given the chance to speak on campus about my paranormal studies by a small student group called IMPACT that had found my work at MinnesotaGhosts.com.

I thought about the invite for a while and eventually decided I should pursue it; it's not every day you are able to say you taught at a college you dropped out of.

As I walked up to the Ostrander Auditorium on the night of the event, I saw a large construction paper poster that announced our event. It read: "Ghost Hunters! Paranormal experiences on campus?" and had a large white blob of what I assumed was a ghost.

I always get a kick out of how others interpret our work and how they mix Halloween décor and art into what we do. It's interesting, because where most people think of ghosts as white, amorphous blobs, I think of them as regular people who have died at some point within their lives.

I walked into the empty conclave of the auditorium and set down my equipment box near the stage. I decided I would go over what I was going to talk about and review my outline while waiting for others to show up. I sat in the third row with my jacket on, a notebook in hand, a pen in mouth, and ideas in my mind.

A few moments later, a young man walked into the auditorium and sat down a few seats away from me. He was awfully early, and like me, he had a notebook in hand and pen in his mouth. We sat in silence for a while and awkwardly thought about why the other was there so early.

Eventually he approached me and asked, "Are you Adam Nori?"

"Yes, I am," I replied with slight confusion.

"I am Jeremiah. I am here to cover you guys for the campus paper," he responded with a sigh of relief. "Do you mind if I ask you a few questions?"

I didn't mind, so we went through with the interview. It is always my pleasure to talk to anyone interested in what I do and why I do it because it allows me to view my work through others' eyes.

After the interview, Jeremiah told me that he would stick around for our presentation, and we casually talked off the record about personal experiences he has had in his life that he believed might be paranormal.

It was about this time when my team started to trickle into the auditorium as well as some members of the IMPACT organization. The event began shortly after; about one hundred people were in the audience.

It is always a nervous experience when you start to talk to a large group of strangers about something not many believe in.

When I looked out into this crowd, there was a certain look of disbelief on faces. A lot of people in the audience sat with arms crossed, and to anyone who knows a thing or two about body language, this meant that people were not into what I was talking about.

As I became nervous talking to this crowd, I started to back away from the crowd. As I subconsciously backed away, I bumped into something in the middle of the stage and it pushed me forward. I was afraid I was going to trip over something (like a power cord), so I walked back up towards the front of the stage.

Each time I talk to a crowd of people, I have found that an interesting event always occurs, a social behavior that happens because it is so taboo in our culture to talk about experiences many believe to be associated with ghosts and hauntings. People never want to be singled out, labeled as odd, and they always try to fit in with a crowd. Because of this, no one ever wants to be the first to raise his or her hand to share a "crazy" experience with strangers. It is only when a person is brave enough to break the ice that other hands start to raise. On this night, the brave soul came in the form of a nine-year-old girl. She was my saving grace in this difficult moment of the presentation.

"Does anyone have any questions about what has been discussed so far?" I asked nervously into the crowd.

A brief moment of silence came over the auditorium until a small arm shot up, seeming to create a sonic boom.

"Yes! You there, what question do you have?" I asked with haste. I was excited that someone raised a hand and could feel the pressure of tension in the room start to drop.

"Is it normal for your cupboard doors to open in your kitchen by themselves?" the young girl asked as she stood up.

"No, that is something we hear about a lot in cases. Sometimes it is a way for the ghosts to get your attention," I replied with a higher pitch as most of us do with children.

"Okay!" the young girl exclaimed as she sat down quickly. She seemed rather content with that answer. I was a bit confused but decided to move on with the presentation.

Another hand shot up and asked about how we know it's a ghost and not just a mouse making noise in the house. Then another hand shot up and asked why we don't get paid for what we do. Then another hand! And another! The crowd slowly began to break out of their shell and became confident because of the courage of this one little girl.

She eventually raised her hand again and asked if it was normal to hear footsteps in her attic. I responded that it was not. With a laugh, I asked the girl her address so we could check out the house.

The crowd laughed and the presentation went on without further issue.

After the two-hour presentation, I was exhausted. As usual, each person in the audience had his or her own personal questions they wanted to ask. This created a large mob around our table on the stage. As each person in line approached our team and asked a question, we tried to answer what we could in the time that the IMPACT team allowed them. The questions were normal, such as "Where does one get an EMF detector?" and "Have you guys ever seen the show *Ghost Hunters*?"

All the questions were normal ones we get often, until two women approached me. One woman was in her twenties, the other in her early forties. They explained that the younger one was a student at the college. She heard about our group being at campus on that night and asked the older lady to tag along, because it seemed to be something that would interest her. She explained why they showed up at the event.

"I just wanted to let you know that I am a local psychic from New Ulm. I came to make sure that you guys didn't say anything wrong. You know how some people can ruin things by not knowing anything they are talking about. Well, you guys did a wonderful job and I am relieved because I was nervous," she said.

This older lady turned out to be Mary Kay, the psychic who would help us at the New Ulm Bed and Breakfast mentioned earlier in this book. This event took place a year prior to our investigation and was the start of our friendship.

As I have mentioned earlier, I prefer objective evidence uncontaminated by human interaction. Due to this perspective, I was short with her because normally I don't put much faith in people who openly claim to be psychic. She must have picked up on my attitude, because then she dropped the bombshell of all bombshells on me.

"I also wanted to let you know that you weren't alone up on that stage. There were two spirits up there with you. One was an older lady in a Victorian dress who wasn't really aware of your team. She kept pacing on the stage behind you."

"The other was an older gentleman who was short and round. He had a brown beard and kept clapping his hands saying how proud he was of you, Adam. He was behind you the whole time, and at one point, you even bumped into him."

Epilogue

It is often said it is the journey, not the destination, that is the reward. In many senses, my excursion into the unknown, the places I found myself in, and the people I met were the final gift from Bobby.

In the end, each of us has to find our own spot in the world. My uncle had many friends; he could drive for hours and find a home with company to welcome him. Through my voyage of trying to find him, my ultimate discovery was that my own life began to mirror his.

I often wonder if there is such a thing as fate but always find myself too lost for an answer. Was that day in 1995 supposed to happen so I would end up where I was today? What made me so aware as to promise to find my uncle in the afterlife? Why did I form such a strong bond with someone who was in my life for such a short time?

These are questions I may never answer, but perhaps things happen for a reason. Each meeting in our life is made to have significance beyond what we can understand at that moment.

I continue to walk in the dark, trying to find others as lost as I am, hoping we make brief contact—whether it's a short recording of sometimes-inaudible words or a fleeting glimpse of a shadow walking across my path.

We often look at ghosts with fear because we don't understand them, yet we barely take the time to understand ourselves and the ones around us. I find it quite ironic. Perhaps those who are brave enough to venture out into the darkness are the ones who truly know what it means to be alive?

Several years removed from my uncle, I find myself understanding exactly just how short life is. I am at the crossroads of my own life, where things like family, career, and legacy become important words. I have spent many years searching out those who regret their own decisions in life and yearn for one more chance at breathing.

I don't want my life to be theirs.

Yet, my life has been made of darkness, shadows, strange technology, and the historical stories of those who used to be. I find comfort in being able to speak for those who cannot. I find value in telling stories that have been forgotten.

I understand my destination, a place where we all end up sooner or later, but more importantly, I know that I can appreciate the journey.

We all should.

Acknowledgments

The Departed

This book would not be possible without the deceased I have met along the way. Whether it was a set of young girls who wanted to play hide-and-seek at a museum or a spirit who replied to my attempt at an EVP with humor, each and every one I met along the way was unique and left a lasting impact on my life. It is only right that these forgotten souls receive first honor in this book.

All the Clients I've Met Along the Way

There have been some truly amazing times etched upon my soul by each one of you. I have seen a wonderful transformation of a shy, quiet, and scared museum curator turn into a spectral disciplinarian. I have met a lady who was so grateful that she took down all her emotional walls to say thank you—which took me by surprise. I have met a family in Sauk Centre whose bond formed on a soulful level. Ultimately, I have made many friends from a fateful random selection of strangers. That is what it means to be blessed. I am grateful for each one of you.

Robert Lusti

"Good night everybody and be kind" summed up so much. Missed by many but not forgotten.

Kristin

Through long hours of writing this book and being a partner in documenting these stories, words cannot sum up what odd things we have been through. Thank you for putting up with all the crazy adventures I led us to.

Mickey

The first time I met you, you found out what I did. It didn't take long to ask to come along "just one night" and today I find you with the same spark of curiosity I began with. I think sometimes you wonder if you bit off more than you can chew, but you understand deep down why you do it. Don't ever lose that!

Monica

You were the first to push me and help guide the MNPSG in a right direction as a case manager. You did more for this organization than I think even you know! I know you miss the "action" but not as much as I miss the days investigating southern Minnesota with you.

Kelly

You were the second part punch of the dynamic duo with Monica. I knew you two could always get a case figured out and scheduled in a way that worked for everyone. I never knew how lucky I was to have your talents in the beginning; meeting new people in a cemetery just hasn't been the same.

Nancy W.

All I can say is that you were quite the firecracker, but I am grateful for all you did. You were the first person who showed me that being straightforward and honest was a virtue that was learned, not earned.

Garrett S.

When no one else in our circle of friends understood what solace a cemetery could bring, you did…even if it meant it was a raccoon-infested, eyes-glowing-in-the-dark kind of situation that would make anyone cringe. What were we thinking?!

Jim S.

The original tech guy. The crazy things you came up with! I will never understand your thinking pattern for technology, but I definitely appreciate it! Thank you for thinking outside of the box.

Don L.

I appreciated that every investigation you took on made you like a kid in a candy store. There is so much passion in what you attempt, and it's easy to overlook when it's present; but the true value shows when it's gone. Thank you for pushing the group with new ideas and adventures!

Justin H.

Always the innocent guinea pig for the other members of the MNPSG, I appreciate your sheer willingness to try new things, even if it was getting to bunk with Lucy at the Palmer House Hotel and not knowing the history of events in that room. Being the nice, innocent guy who writes supernatural horror movies, I thank you for the talent and humor you bring to the team.

John S.

As someone I like to refer to as "the Paranormal Godfather," I appreciate all you have done for Minnesota's paranormal history. You have been a true friend and confidant since I started this journey. Thank you for being the crazy, zany, and wacky you!

MNPSG Members, Past and Present

I have had the distinct honor of meeting many of you and understanding that each one of you had been selected for your own personal talents and ambitious endeavors. At the time of writing this book, there have been more than thirty members over the course of two teams, so thanking each one of you would take almost another book! However, I understand that each member drives the team and adds a unique element to the organization, which makes it a very different being than it was before. Without each one of you, the team could not exist.

GET MORE AT LLEWELLYN.COM

Visit us online to browse hundreds of our books and decks, plus sign up to receive our e-newsletters and exclusive online offers.

- Free tarot readings • Spell-a-Day • Moon phases
- Recipes, spells, and tips • Blogs • Encyclopedia
- Author interviews, articles, and upcoming events

GET SOCIAL WITH LLEWELLYN

 Find us on Facebook
www.Facebook.com/LlewellynBooks

Follow us on
www.Twitter.com/Llewellynbooks

GET BOOKS AT LLEWELLYN

LLEWELLYN ORDERING INFORMATION

Order online: Visit our website at www.llewellyn.com to select your books and place an order on our secure server.

Order by phone:
- Call toll free within the U.S. at 1-877-NEW-WRLD (1-877-639-9753)
- Call toll free within Canada at 1-866-NEW-WRLD (1-866-639-9753)
- We accept VISA, MasterCard, and American Express

 Order by mail:
Send the full price of your order (MN residents add 6.875% sales tax) in U.S. funds, plus postage and handling to: Llewellyn Worldwide, 2143 Wooddale Drive Woodbury, MN 55125-2989

POSTAGE AND HANDLING:
STANDARD: (U.S. & Canada)
(Please allow 2 business days)
$25.00 and under, add $4.00.
$25.01 and over, FREE SHIPPING.

INTERNATIONAL ORDERS (airmail only):
$16.00 for one book, plus $3.00 for each additional book.

Visit us online for more shipping options. Prices subject to change.

FREE CATALOG!

To order, call
1-877-NEW-WRLD
ext. 8236
or visit our website

Haunting
experiences

encounters with the otherworldly

Michelle Belanger

From the author of *Walking the Twilight Path*

Haunting Experiences
Encounters with the Otherworldly
MICHELLE BELANGER

Working the graveyard shift at a haunted hotel, encountering a Voodoo spirit in New Orleans, helping the victim of an astral vampire attack…the supernatural has played a part in Michelle Belanger's life since the age of three. Yet she refuses to take the "unexplained" for granted, especially when the dead speak to her.

From haunted violins to dark fey, Belanger relives her thrilling experiences with haunted people, places, and things. Inspired to understand the shadowy truths about these paranormal mysteries, she examines each otherworldly encounter with a skeptical eye. What remains is a solid survey of the paranormal from a credible narrator, who also learns to accept her own gifts for spirit communication.

978-0-7387-1437-0, 264 pp., 6 x 9   **$15.95**

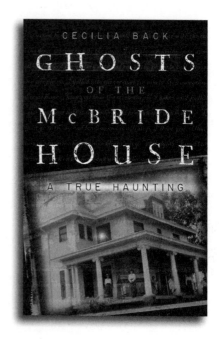

CECILIA BACK

GHOSTS
OF THE
McBRIDE
HOUSE

A TRUE HAUNTING

Ghosts of the McBride House
A True Haunting
Cecilia Back

It took Cecilia Back only a few weeks to confirm that her new home—a Victorian mansion just across the street from a historic military fort—was haunted. But instead of fleeing, the Back family stayed put and gradually got to know their "spirited" residents over the next twenty-five years.

Meet Dr. McBride, the original owner who loves scaring away construction crews and the author's ghost-phobic mother. Try to catch sight of the two spirit children who play with Back's son and daughter and loud, electronic toys in the middle of the night. Each ghost has a personality of its own, including one transient entity whose antics are downright terrifying.

Despite mischievous pranks, such as raucous ghost parties at two a.m., the Back family have come to accept—and occasionally welcome—these unique encounters with the dead.

978-0-7387-1505-6, 216 pp., 5³⁄₁₆ x 8   **$14.95**

The Sallie House Haunting
A True Story
Debra Pickman

Who knew that our experience would push us over the edge of disbelief and through the door of certain terror?

Debra Pickman had always wanted a ghost of her own. She never expected her wish to come horrifically true when she, her husband, and their newborn son moved into a century-old home in Atchison, Kansas, that—to their shock—is also occupied by a fire-starting spirit child named Sallie … and darker, aggressive forces.

Gradually, Debra becomes attached to Sallie and adjusts to her ghostly mischief—toys turning on by themselves, knick-knacks moving, and electrical disruptions. But serious problems arise when she can't control Sallie's habit of lighting fires. What's worse, her husband Tony becomes the victim of scratches, bites, and terrifying ghostly attacks that are clearly the work of other menacing entities. Discover how the ongoing terror takes its toll on their nerves, sanity, and marriage, and what finally forces the Pickmans to flee the infamous Sallie House.

978-0-7387-2128-6, 288 pp., 6 x 9   **$16.95**

---

a
true
story

The
Ghosts
on
87th
Lane

M. L. Woelm

The Ghosts on 87th Lane
A True Story
M. L. Woelm

After moving her young family into their first house—a small suburban home in the Midwest—a series of strange and chilling events take place: unexplained noises, objects disappearing, lights going out by themselves, phantom footsteps. And then M. L. Woelm's neighbor confirms the horrifying truth: her house is haunted.

Beginning in 1968 and spanning three decades, this moving memoir chronicles the hair-raising episodes that nearly drove an ordinary housewife and mother to the breaking point. With friends who thought she was crazy and a skeptical, unsupportive husband who worked nights, the author was left all alone in her terror. How did she cope with disembodied sobs, eerie feelings of being watched, mysterious scratches appearing on her throat, and a phantom child's voice crying "Mommy!" in her ear?

Discover how frazzled nerves and constant stress wreak havoc on the author's health and marriage, until she finally finds validation and understanding from ghost expert Echo Bodine, friends, her grown children, and finally…her husband.

978-0-7387-1031-0, 288 pp., 6 x 9   **$12.95**

How to be a Ghost Hunter
Richard Southall

So you want to investigate a haunting? This book is full of
practical advice used in the author's own ghost hunting prac-
tice. Find out whether you're dealing with a ghost, spirit, or
an entity...and discover the one time when you should stop
what you're doing and call in an exorcist. Learn the four-
phase procedure for conducting an effective investigation,
how to capture paranormal phenomena on film, record disembodied sounds and voices on tape, assemble an affordable
ghost-hunting kit, and form your own paranormal group.

For anyone with time and little money to spend on equipment, this book will help you maintain a healthy sense of skepticism and thoroughness while you search for authentic evidence of the paranormal.

978-0-7387-0312-1, 168 pp., 5³⁄₁₆ x 8   **$12.95**

Is Your House Haunted?
Poltergeists, Ghosts or Bad Wiring
DEBI CHESTNUT

A door slams shut by itself, pets are acting strangely, inexplicable smells and sounds are invading your home … and you're terrified. Is there a logical explanation, or do you have a real-life ghost on your hands?

There's no reason to live in fear. This no-nonsense beginner's guide offers reassurance and practical advice on identifying—and putting a stop to—any paranormal activity that's creeping you out. Discover how to rule out any earthly explanations for strange phenomena. A comprehensive overview of all kinds of hauntings and ghosts—from aggressive poltergeists to harmless family spirits to malevolent demons—will help you understand and identify your unearthly houseguest. If you still want to banish your ghost, you'll find plenty of simple, effective techniques to get the job done.

978-0-7387-2681-6, 240 pp., 5³⁄₁₆ x 8　　　　**$14.95**

True Casefiles of a
Paranormal Investigator
Stephen Lancaster

As a ghost hunter for nearly fifteen years, Stephen Lancaster's encounters with the paranormal range from the merely incredible to the downright terrifying. This gripping collection of true casefiles takes us behind the scenes of his most fascinating paranormal investigations.

See what it's like to come face to face with an unearthly glowing woman in a dark cemetery, be attacked by invisible entities, talk to spirits using a flashlight, and dodge objects launched by a poltergeist. Every delicious detail is documented: the history and legends of each haunted location, what Stephen's thinking and feeling throughout each unimaginable encounter, and how he manages to capture ghost faces, spirit voices, a cowboy shadow man, otherworldly orbs, a music-loving spirit playing an antique piano, and other extraordinary paranormal evidence.

978-0-7387-3220-6, 240 pp., 5³⁄₁₆ x 8   **$15.95**
